# SOCIAL WARFARE

## CULTIVATING A REVOLUTION FOR A NATION UNDER SIEGE

# MATTHEW GEDDIE

# SOCIAL WARFARE: CULTIVATING A REVOLUTION FOR A NATION UNDER SIEGE

1405 SW 6th Avenue • Ocala, Florida 34471 • Phone 352-622-1825 • Fax 352-622-1875
Website: www.atlantic-pub.com • Email: sales@atlantic-pub.com
SAN Number: 268-1250

The opinions expressed in our published works are those solely of the author and do not reflect the opinions of Atlantic Publishing Group, Inc. (referred to as publisher) or its editors.

Library of Congress Control Number: 2019053846

Printed in the United States

INTERIOR LAYOUT AND JACKET DESIGN: Nicole Sturk

# TABLE OF CONTENTS

# CHAPTER 1
# VERSATILITY

**M**ost tragedy in this world is caused by people who want to change things because they feel they can improve situations. They don't always want to intentionally disrupt or cause damage. But if damage should occur in the process, they can't see themselves ever being affected simply because they are preoccupied with being right about themselves.

We all allow ourselves to be influenced in different ways to certain circumstances. It's important not to become a monolithic thinker. Sometimes we have to ask ourselves, 'if I'm not for myself, who will be? And if I'm only for myself, what am I?' We can speed up or slow down our own demise when we think the obverse is impossible. We should never lose touch with our inner self.

The theatre of the mind is an outlet for rage, and a person has to have a balancing point. Rage is a single emotion and some people have a theatrical gene. People are always trying to assess their own loss through their emotions, so they isolate things by subject matter. Any action we take always has an equal reaction, so people tend to create their own identity when they make their own level of perception through social cohesion.

People are usually quick to say that they are well informed until someone drops a bomb of cognitive dissonance on them. Everything we see and hear around us sets the tone. Everything is about time. We live in a world where people have learned to love their chemically induced servitude. We often never see an opportunity to restore our pride until someone else is omitted. A person is born with nuance in order to know right from wrong.

This is why it becomes necessary sometimes to reinvent ourselves, and by doing so, we find new avenues for success. The struggle itself is the success. But when it comes too quickly, it's usually more of a curse than a blessing, and in the end, it's always a stale finale. Everything is superseded by complex social engineering, clearing the way for structural change to continue forward.

There is an underlying physical world that can't be explained. What we do, in many ways, becomes our own salvation. Much like the builder is to the building or the painter is to the painting, one could not have existed without the other. Brevity is indeed the sister of talent. As Werner Heisenberg so aptly noted in his uncertainty principle, we live in a time where the greater risk for tragedy lies in conflict of two rights rather than right and wrong. It is ultra-tolerance alone that is polluting the world.

People no longer take a moral picture of their surroundings. We as a society have become programmed, through social engineering, with a technique called neuro-linguistic programming where we're all told how to think, how to feel, and how to act. We are products of our environment because we have been wired that way without even realizing it.

Emotional resistance will always emerge and can never be set aside like false ideas and ignorance can. If a nation, like a ship, allows itself to veer off course by one degree, and no one is at the helm to charter the destination, we must ask where we will end up when we finally, if ever, get back to land. A land that we no longer recognize from what it once was. Our errors are portals into unexplored regions. Most of the information that we already have was acquired by looking for something and finding something else along the way.

# CHAPTER 2
# TRUTH

The best recipe for success is the remedy for failure, which usually requires self-denial and hard work. Most people only want to go with what's easier and more fashionable. A dialogue is created when you start telling the truth and people start hating you. They've heard lies for so long, they are used to eating it and they don't want anything else because it tastes bad, so they reject it. This has been said many times, but the truth is stranger than fiction. In the society we live, we should develop an interest in life as we see it in the people, places, and things that require us to use our mind and not just focus on the here and now.

Also, what may become reality because reality is the truth and we should always look at what may be ahead. If we fail to plan, we plan to fail and don't even realize it when looking at what may become the truth on the horizon. By doing that we take a responsible approach to the future, and that gives us merit, dignity, and worth to what will be history.

# CHAPTER 3
# APPEASEMENT

Everyone should be an observer of nature to some degree. There comes a point in human evolution when we have to take a look at what evolves around us, whether it's diabolical or something we see as benign. Ignorance is bliss until the consequences arrive. Passion is an emotion that equals focus, action, direction, and destination. It can easily turn into an obsession when not controlled.

Truth to power is a revolutionary act when other people want to bring down the conventional way of life. Somebody somewhere always seems to think they know how the system works and knows a better way. The first thing they do is apply a scarlet letter to everything that doesn't fit their narrative. We're not supposed to just accept how someone else defines reality without first knowing all the facts. Just because someone accepts something by saying it's what they wanted doesn't mean it's what is best.

There are dispositions in human beings that can always be broken: the mind, body, and soul. We have the abstraction of our own human social life and the way we behave. We have to retain our own individual will as we retain our own entity. Sometimes it seems that everything is antithetical to what we believe. People—now more than ever—have a victim mentality. The problem is that there will always be a sublime person more than willing to stir up the poor and disenfranchised, saying that it's because of the people who do have things that they are kept at a disadvantage. It makes it necessary for someone to be a gatekeeper of the truth and determine what's real and what's not.

All our interior world, by and large, is about keeping people silent. People are kept at a disadvantage by the dissemination of information. People love to blame their failures on external factors because they've become blinded by their own ambition. Just because an opposing team has more yards on the field does not mean they are going to win the game. It's how many points they put on the board at the end.

All wars are based on deception, motive, and opportunity. When we're near, make them think we're far; when we're far, make them think we're near. Avoid what is strong and strike at what is weak. We succeed at places we attack when they are left undefended. Appeasement only emboldens an aggressor, so as a defense mechanism we ridicule irony and expose the folly of other people. Very few wars have ended with things staying the same as when they started. If we allow ourselves to become a tempest in a teapot, there's no way to conserve the biodiversity of our ecosystem.

In order to find self-fulfillment, people have to expose themselves to new opportunities through art. When we apply our skills to newfound opportunity, we find talent. It's not enough to just be gifted or talented at something. The real achievement is having the courage to follow our talent into the dark places it may lead us into.

# CHAPTER 4
# SUCCESS

It is true that success is always better when we achieve it without destroying our principles. That doesn't change the fact that, in many cases, our success will mean someone else's failure. But that doesn't mean that we have to let go of our integrity or our principles.

Success is peace of mind, which is a direct result of the self-satisfaction in knowing you made the effort to do the best of which you are capable. Many times in life, people find out that they don't achieve the success they desire, not because their aim is too high and they miss, but because their aim is too low and they reach it. They end up staying right there because they don't want change.

One formula for success is to under-promise and over-deliver, and in doing so, we can raise the bar in our own mind. But many times we neglect to do so and it's because of our own trepidation. When we set out to achieve something, it's always a good mindset to be the change we wish to see. Most people don't want change of any type. In fact, people fear change more than anything in the world. Naturally, people usually have a negative view of change, but, in truth, change is a good thing more often than not. It's hard to keep up progress without change because the world is always evolving. We should remember that progress is a nice word but change is its motivator.

# CHAPTER 5
# OPPORTUNITY CHANGE

In reference to opportunity, we often fail to realize that we have become a society of introverts who are only concerned with our own thoughts. We're so caught up in ourselves that we can't see that it's best to act on what we have, even if what we have is not exactly what we want. Being prudent is a good thing, but we shouldn't lose sight of what we have and resist the overwhelming desire for self-gratification. If we wait too long to act on something, there may not be any good options left to choose from. After we make a careful examination of the facts, we must never let ourselves forget that facts do not cease to exist just because they are ignored. Facts are stubborn things, and it's in our nature to ignore them.

When we are caught up in our ambition, whatever that may be, we have the mindset that we need a chemical vacation from an intolerable world. We're looking for our artificial sedation or inspiration and all the while letting every opportunity that comes our way just pass us by for the simple reason that we don't want to change. We want to stay in what we think is our comfort zone. We don't even realize that we're looking into the abyss, and the abyss is looking right back into us.

*Wisdom consists in being able to distinguish among dangers and make a choice of the least harmful.*

—Niccole Machiavelli

# CHAPTER 6
# IMPULSE

Every thought we have has a counter thought, and everyone always seems to do what they feel like doing. The fact is that human beings are very complex. The worst thing that anyone can do is go through their whole life playing the victim because there are several dimensions to every person. Everybody has duality in how they think, feel, and act; there always seems to be a fight in the inner self of a person. People who repress their thoughts or ideas always seem to put themselves at a disadvantage by making an existing problem even worse. We should accept what we're thinking and feeling without always acting on it.

One difference between a sane person and an insane person is not what they think but what they do. With that being said, we can look back on our errors as portals of discovery and stop blaming ignorance on misfortune. There comes a time in almost everyone's life when we have to look at cause and effect and start looking at the reason why.

# CHAPTER 7
# LOGIC

Poverty is not a vice and affluence is not virtue, and to think otherwise would be remiss. We should be aware of anyone who preaches fairness for all because there is no such thing and to say that there is only distorts reality. You can use pure logic and reach more people; using what is factual will only give credence and strength to your message. A time will come when we have to have some semblance of reality. We eventually have to acknowledge it for what it is and ask ourselves if we want it, as it's not going to go away but will always be there.

We spend so much time and wasted energy getting to a place high on a mountain, and we soon find out that it's not at all where we want to be. We went through all that needless effort to roll a boulder up the mountain without even realizing that it will be more difficult to walk it back down the other side.

We have to look at where we've placed ourselves in life and figure out the best way to come down to the valley of reality in order to survive and do what we can when our survival is at stake. We can try to reinvent ourselves and become someone we're not, but the same personality that we've always had will eventually emerge; to think otherwise would be disingenuous. In our quest for prosperity, we should remember that it is only an instrument to be used and not a deity to be worshiped.

# CHAPTER 8
# SELF-PRESERVATION

It's not always about how much we commit to memory, or what we know. It's more about being able to separate what we do know from what we don't know. An argument does not validate the truth. It simply tells someone what may be real. We already have it in us to combat what's not real. However we let people and things in that we didn't want in. Then things happen that we didn't want to happen. We live in a culture that honors and prides itself in shifting blame to other people. This decay has become a symbol of virtue and intellect in modern society.

Self-reproach has become almost nonexistent in today's world. A person has to learn to look beyond the realm of the inner self. What works in our personal life may not always work in the real world mostly because we don't have the same comforts we're accustomed to having. We need to recognize what's happening and learn to define the moment before it defines us.

People have learned to form their opinion by going with the mainstream narrative and what's fashionable. This causes an upheaval in our lives whether we like it or not. It's easy to recognize the ideals of a society by its public expressions, so it's necessary to advance from a passive voice to an active voice. When we want people to listen to advice, it's better to make them think that it's their own advice. It usually takes time to persuade people to do something, even if it's for their own good. Often people have to be convinced before they can be committed to something. The only thing that's easy for everyone to agree on is something that no one has interest in. That makes it necessary to learn the text before we ever give the commentary. Only by changing a demographic can a nation of people be changed. When we enter into this arena, it is very important not to become overzealous. When we are overzealous, we go too far too fast and there are unintended consequences.

Science, by definition, is open to new discoveries. However most adventures never reach their predetermined end simply because people fail to follow through. It is usually fear that makes someone hesitant to advise other people when it has become the norm for most of them to ignore advice altogether. It's important to realize that we can't spin the world in whatever direction we want. Instead, we must learn to make the necessary adjustments, then get out of the way when we determine the direction. A person can only feel inferior by their acceptance of this emotion. We've become a society of complacent people, lacking significant interest in everyday events and activities. People have become loyal only to trivia in their daily lives. When do we set goals and take aim at what we want, we eventually have to take action. The average person has a difficult time explaining exactly what they want, so they need someone else to express it for them. Then, with an aggrieved face, they are willing to face any adversity to get what someone else decided they need. This is the big lie that's heard around the world and fed upon greedily in a free and open society.

We should remember that the greater the lie, the more likely people are to believe it. It has become common practice for people to believe only what they prefer to be true and what they hope is true. Typically, people are angry at what they have done to themselves. It usually fuels their anger to see content in someone else. They often need to be poked with the sharp stick of reality. When we wake up one day and find that we have to crawl on one arm and one leg, then by all means, we should crawl on one arm and one leg.

# CHAPTER 9
# REALITY

Our entire world is reality and certainly more so than our apparent world. Once you cleanse the doors of perception, you can most often see reality for what it is. People usually don't want to face reality simply because it's not what they want it to be, but we should keep in mind that realism is not always cynicism, no matter what our perception of something may be and what we believe. Facts don't cease to exist because they are ignored. It's not uncommon for people to ignore facts just because they don't like what they are. Many times in life when we ask for advice, we already know the answer but wish we didn't.

Statistics show that things tend to work out much better if we approach a problem with an open mind, not an open mouth, and face reality even when we think it's meaningless to do so. Doing what we can with what we have where we are makes sense because waiting for more options usually results in having fewer or no options at all.

# CHAPTER 10
# EGOISM

Everyone has triggers that can set off the way they behave. No one wants to be reviled by someone who thinks they're smarter or better than they are. Anyone with any self-esteem wants to be revered in one way or another; anyone who has pride in themselves is, to some extent, egotistical, and that's okay. Anyone who wants someone else to abandon their ego usually wants something that someone else has and are angry because they don't have anything to be egotistical about. So, in many ways, people will try to triangulate and marginalize someone within their own reality with some sort of dialogue, so we should never allow ourselves to become a transparent person whom anyone can look straight through.

Our lives are defined by moments we never see coming. With that being said, a person should never live in fear. People should live in hope, because in every walk of life, there are good and bad people in every group. One of the worst things a person can do is define themselves by the bad things that may have happened to them in life and then use that to go around playing the victim. By doing so, they will live a miserable life, so there has to be a rational discourse in order to preserve their sanity.

It's true that no matter where we go or what we do in life we live entirely within the confines of our own mind, and we always seem to waste a lot of time running after people, places, and things that we could have caught just by standing still. It's a simple truth that God exists whether we choose to believe it or not, and yet we continue to argue about who's right and who's wrong.

A person should adapt to what's been given to them and use whatever they have to succeed in life. As far as reality goes, we can continue to talk about what's true and what's false, but ultimately, most people find reality when it knocks them down. That's because people are generally misinformed about reality, opting to stick to the textbook version.

We live our life going up or down—no one remains static. We're always going one way or another, and time is something that we leave a small mark on as we pass through. We often struggle our entire life to achieve what we think we want to be or to attain and we usually end up feeling crushed if and when we get there. Success is a stale finale simply because most people are never satisfied with what they have or aspire to be.

In the final analysis, something is or is not an element. In simple chemistry, when broken down you either have it or you don't, but too many times we choose to believe part and parcel of a lie. We want to believe we can acquire something that's simply not there and that is beyond our reach.

# CHAPTER 11
# IRONY

A person's resistance is usually activated by their own despair. The truth that many people never understand until it's too late, is the more they try to avoid suffering, the more they suffer. That's because insignificant things begin to torment them in proportion to their fear of being hurt. Not everyone is adapted to the same things in life, therefore it can be important to follow the basic building blocks of society. One of the most basic, most important rules in science is to always reduce things to their simplest terms in order to understand what's going on. We often find ourselves resigned to our own fate by accepting plans that are no longer relevant.

It has been said that irony is the hygiene of the mind and human nature is largely something that has to be overcome. Having said that, when we want to achieve something, there will come a time when we have to learn to walk alone or risk getting the opposite of what we expected. Our society has become devoid of values, and lies are more acceptable. It's usually the people that we are most opposed to that help drive us in a different direction and intensify our energy as we go.

Life's reality is not always being sure, not knowing what's next or how to proceed. Sometimes we have to guess at the expense of being wrong. At the perimeters of understanding there is no art. We find ourselves having to take a leap into the dark, out into the unknown. If a person spends their entire life being afraid of a storm, they can never learn to sail their own ship. In the final analysis, once we expose ourselves to our fears, we soon find that fear has no power and vanishes. In order to be successful, a person has to have the maturity to endure a certain degree of uncertainty in life.

# CHAPTER 12
# SOCIAL AWARENESS

A retrospective analysis confirms that all scientific knowledge is open to challenge at any time. The same can be said about the assessment of the world in general. How we are doing as a whole could be a philosophy unto itself. Nearly everyone has the opportunity to model their philosophy by their own actions. The problem is that most of the people don't want to be confused with facts because their mind is made up. It's easy for someone to hear a message without hearing its content.

There's always a huge audience that hates something they don't understand. It's the same audience that says to forgive — until it becomes their turn. Reality should always be at the heart of any civil society. Since Neolithic times, the natural state of any human is fear and anxiety. It's something that few people have learned to overcome. Instead, people want to repress their emotions and then substitute their inadequacy for hatred.

Repressed aggression is depression. Anger falls one letter short of danger. The only way to channel it successfully is to be a productive and active participant in something we find beneficial. What we often think is an ideal situation may be fine, but reality is better. When it comes to reality versus anything else, the fight is over—reality wins every time. We're all part of the human condition, and we're all going to lose at some point in our lives. There is nothing that doesn't cost someone something.

No nation was ever forged in peace. Every nation has stolen from another through observation, extermination, and occupation. Any society can quickly go from a silent majority to a silenced majority with little resistance. There has always been two kinds of people: active participants and passive consumers. Internal disintegration and decay will only postpone demise and won't halt the inevitable.

All nations, cultures, traditions, and beliefs are not the same. Yet the world somehow continues to converge. Believing and seeing are both often wrong and having belief through faith is more often than not a rational thing to have. More often than not, when we don't know where we're going, we end up on the wrong end of something or somewhere we don't want to be. Because we live in a blame culture, people want to blame their circumstances and condition on the environment in which they've placed themselves.

A foreign country is not designed to make the traveler comfortable. We're not designed to feel indigenous everywhere we go. By expecting people to be congenial in any society, we're expecting too much. It's irrational and not even within reach of the modern world. In all of creation, humans are the only ones who are surprised at what is expected to happen. When all goes silent, it should be obvious that everyone else is listening for a reason.

# CHAPTER 13
# INDIVIDUALISM

People have an imaginary view of the world and do not want to accept the fact that they're not going to mold the world into their own image. So we develop our own idealization and want something that never will be simply because we don't want to accept our own dissatisfaction. Our mind travels, traverses, and transcends because we have an oppressive air and we feel that we have to like something or do something just because other people are doing it.

In all reality, the thoughts that we choose to act upon define us to others, and the thoughts we do not act upon define us to ourselves. Therefore, many times we find that our errors become portals of discovery. No two people are the same, so having our own likes and dislikes that are unique as opposed to others' is all well and good, providing that we do not overly force our dialogue or view. This is called tempering through mind mapping technique.

A creative mind can take a disagreement and turn it into something good. So, we should try and find our own harmony based on something other than what we want in the here and now and realize that the first rule of science is that there is no absolute. Therefore, anything that's not absolute offers no consensus of opinion. When it comes to defining the observation, the argument is over and there is no room to invest our entire premise built on what may be a lie, and most rational people don't want to build on that because they're afraid that the truth may come out and all credibility would be lost. Just because someone has good intentions doesn't mean that they're always going to do something good, and if that's the case, their actions are usually followed by unintended and sometimes fatal consequences.

A person doesn't have to be an expert in a certain field to have the mental capacity to understand the literature. In fact, some of the greatest things ever accomplished by some of the best minds of our time were by people who did not yield to trends, fads, and popular opinion. With that said, when someone does find their own realization, they also have to find their own level of intensity or else their ideology may run amuck...

# CHAPTER 14
# SELF-REPROACH

One of the greatest challenges that any human can face is to go from an immortal mentality to a mortal mentality. The best way to get rid of something is to reverse-engineer its creation. Instead of being a dilettante, a person must go through a complete reformation. We live in the human condition and in the human condition, some rise and some fall. Still, people want more and more because we live in a consumer society.

It's impossible to make everything equal because we don't live in an equal society. When all someone has is fanaticism, they eventually end up with nothing. There's no way to make the outcome equal to the human spirit.

The human spirit wants to be better than the other by being competitive. Society can't be reinvented to their worldly view. Not everyone has the greed and the hunger to prove that they're better than the next man who doesn't have the greed gene. It's always these people who are so willing to do irrational things in the pursuit of a payoff.

Even in an affluent society, the logic never seems to satisfy. They put the ideology before the facts and it places a hold on them. Nothing else is even remotely interesting. When people allow themselves to be driven this way, they don't want to hear otherwise. They know they are right and do not have the time for competing views. Since the beginning, mankind has been trying to use the outer world to reflect the inner-world self. With a convergence of energy, people have learned to create things in spite of their neurosis, whether it's a positive or a negative, and that is what inspires people.

We are a part of a society where nearly everyone thinks that they are correct in their assumptions and that what they have to say is important. What most people don't understand is how pathetically little difference it makes to the outcome. No matter how much someone wants to believe that the end will justify the means, it doesn't make it so.

Science and innovation are always open to new discoveries — that's why there are no absolutes. A few hundred years ago, 98 percent of the world thought the Earth was flat. Belief and fact have to remain at a distance in order to advance the human condition. There are a few people in the world who know how to make something work and can watch someone else do it incorrectly but not interfere. The ones who are determined to make life unpleasant for everyone else are some of the most miserable people on Earth. The most volatile people in existence are the ones who think they are suffering for what they believe to be true.

When a person eats something that's bad, the stomach usually ejects it. The human brain can and often does hold onto things no matter how distasteful they may be. More often these days people choose to let their mind hold and absorb what they know is rotten. Then the person slowly becomes septic from their own indulgence.

A fish always rots from the head down—the same concept applies to people. It all starts at the top. A miserable idea has to be thought of before it can be taught. We don't have the ability to correlate all the contents of our mind. We do however, have the ability to enter in only what we allow.

The most insignificant people in the world are the ones most apt to smear others. Change is the law of progress and usually is our greatest ally. Anyone who constantly defends what they've done wrong has no intention of stopping or changing.

# CHAPTER 15
# RELIEF OF EMOTIONS THROUGH ART

Tragedy is a conflict between human will and fate. Society must be organized around it if we're to persevere. Aristotle, who based his theory of prosperity on the works of Athenian tragedians, said that tragedy should move the reader or spectator to pity and terror, performing a catharsis of the emotions. I can express to you pain, pleasure, tragedy, or calamitous fate all in one topic.

I may not have the answer to all herein, but I certainly have the questions, and that's where a topic begins. Everything starts with a question and usually ends with another question. If you can learn to read the literature, you can know what's being done. Deductive reasoning is all anyone really needs to find an answer. The conclusion will then follow the premise. It's a matter of breaking something down to see what's actually there.

There, however, is the burning question that remains. Have the once-logical people become so disconnected that they can no longer see reality of what is occurring? Or has reality become such an unpleasant burden that they're no longer willing to acknowledge what's transpired? The answer is that it's much of both. To get an understanding of what's going on, you have to stop, look, and listen to what's happening from every direction, not in just one area.

There's nothing new about the propaganda you hear. It has been around since the Stone Age in one form or another. To get a better mental image, you have to look at the entire apparatus. Otherwise you will never know the real cause of something. You would only know the effect it is having, and that alone is useless. You don't necessarily have to know how something happens to know what's making it happen.

The problem people have is that they can't see the reality because they've blocked it out. They are so occupied with their own thoughts that they've simply forgotten how to notice what's happening around them. People seem to be more defiant now than ever, so nihilism is spinning fast.

Tolerance is the last virtue a dying society holds onto. This is primarily why ancient Rome fell the way it did. Diversity and tolerance led to civil unrest, then civil unrest led to civil disobedience, which led to civil war in the midst of the already-constant wars that were taking place. Then came currency manipulation and confiscation of wealth. After being invaded by the Huns, the eastern and the western part split in half and eventually the west collapsed.

Never think that that can't happen here. If you think that it can't, you don't know history. If left unchecked and no one listens to what the seer says, it will come. Whether it's directly or indirectly won't matter. The fact is that society has a distorted view of what tolerance and empathy should be. Now, this time while the fiddle plays, Rome will not be the only thing that will burn—it will be all of Western Civilization.

# CHAPTER 16
# APPLICATION OF COMPROMISE

ituational awareness starts with the senses. When we put our ideology ahead of our survival, we are asleep to the necessities. What you choose to believe is between you and your sensibilities. A sensibility is the ability to feel things mentally and having the ability to respond to a sensory stimulus; it does not mean to have the possession of good sense. Anytime we allow our situational awareness to be overpowered by our ideology, we put our survival in jeopardy. Therefore, when giving an orderly description of events relating to, or having the form of, a narrative, a person generally wants to promote the growth and development of that of which they're supportive. In order to successfully represent a course of action, you have to understand what that action is.

For vanity's sake, when we're able to communicate, it means that we're getting through. There has to be self-confidence and that requires at least some degree of preparation. The outcome will always depend on how the content is presented. People need a meaningful individual responsibility. It gives them a sense of belonging. No matter how meaningful it may be, there has to be an incentive involved. It takes only one or two picking up a crumb of curiosity to ignite the minds of those around them. It's a tested method that's as old as time itself. When people can't come to terms with reality for vanity's sake, it's because they have not learned the art of compromise.

Human beings are compelled to believe everything they see for practical purposes and most of what they hear for convenience. They are blind to what is essential until they no longer have it. What is commonly thought to be irrelevant is often redundant and dangerous. A bell cannot be un-rung once it tolls. In other words, people cannot un-hear what they've already heard, nor can they un-see what they've already seen. They do, however, have the ability to un-think what they've already thought.

Being instrumentally clever in language is an art in itself. Not only do words matter, but how they are projected determines their impact. Being loud about what you want someone to think but also with what they are already thinking will bring solidarity. Pity is unnatural to the human condition. It's a learned behavior that may be added or taken away at any given moment. When we're overly existential, we become self-defeating and nature often revolts amid the struggle. Since reality will not go away, you have to find a way to make the bitter taste a little more palatable.

It's essential to design and match the appetite of whom you're serving. Then, the question that should have been asked takes precedence, rather than the one that was asked. All content must have limitations. When you continue to say things only for personal advantage you will eventually forget what you actually believe. There must be a display of genuine concern for the structures of society. Anytime you're dealing with the development and organization of people with a common interest, they are more inclined to affirm what is actually happening. When cause and effect are more evident by revealing only what is suggestive and not what's vital, creates a mental process where people are more susceptible to the influence and opinion being given. That in itself will eventually result in the acceptance of beliefs arising from a source that will stimulate emotion. Society is responsible and everyone is suspect.

Preconceived ideas are a meaningless effort to try and regulate reality when there is no ideal condition. The ultimate goal must be to think creatively on schedule and raise the ranks of nobility. There's a big difference between a defeatist and a realist. A defeatist will mentally accept defeat before the event occurs, making defeat much more likely. Their judgment is influenced by feeling rather than fact; therefore, they are ruled by emotion rather than reason.

A realist knows that objects of perception have real existence outside the mind. They are more influenced by facts and what's practical as opposed to an emotional reaction. There has to be an element of emotional resistance somewhere, otherwise we'd just live inside our own mind. As a result, there would be no fidelity to life as perceived and experienced through art, philosophy, literature, etc.

We live in a reactionary society that has adopted the pleasure principle, where the moral rightness and the justification of an action are determined by its ability to satisfy human wants. It defines its contribution to the greatest good to the greatest number, no matter the consequence. A reaction is the equal or opposing force, which is always called into play by another force. When the opposing factions are so locked into a predicament that the language barrier can't be broken directly or indirectly and where the relational formation is so resistant and immovable, they must be lead to affirm something that will reveal the absurdity of their own position. That's often followed by consequential damage brought on by one's own action.

The art of compromise is a course of action. It's often a means to settle a dispute by bringing a person or people into danger by their own accord. In order for someone to better understand their current state, they must know how to read the data, though not necessarily understand the data. It's hard for anyone to find truth on their own, so they usually have to be led through a verbal or written passage of ideas. It is then that a person starts to rise to the level of a higher truth and better understand the laws of reason. Instead we are seeing a shift in revitalization and we should ask what is tantamount.

If no one collects the wisdom from the ages, if we are blind to the images along the road of life, where do we go? When we can't even see the shadows on the cave wall anymore, what are we left with?

# CHAPTER 17
# ADMITTING TO CHANGE FOR THE BETTER

Whether we care to admit it or not, we're all part of something that we've met in our lifetime. When we meet someone we think is unbiased, it's only because they have the same biases we have. The most bigoted persons are the ones who have no conviction. In nearly all cases, a person only becomes great through struggle. Complication usually leads to obfuscation. More often than not, simplification will lead us to the right answer. All we really need to honestly know is what, when, where and who. Everything becomes history after that, having no sense of history is like having no eyes or ears. Electronic devices are sometimes sealed components and cannot be repaired. There have always been humans with the same configuration.

Pop psychology's most common myth tells us that human beings are basically good; we need more self-esteem and self-worth; we can't love others until we love ourselves; we shouldn't judge anyone and all guilt is bad. It's like a religion that many people go into because they are already broken and sick.

People that go into the business of helping others are often sick themselves. When people think they're right about something, they want to tell everyone else to believe it also. Then having the freedom and ability to go out and spread this gospel only drives people more. Religion more than anything else is a crutch for people who are not strong enough to stand without help. They love to spend time and money on it, and like a habit, they get considerable pleasure from tinkering with it. It's good medicine for keeping people quiet or for making noise, whichever is needed.

It can be the opium for the masses or the cyanide for a cult. We're all actors and the world's a stage. When we're looking at the live audience of the world, we're really looking at a wild animal. It comes down to verbal arts and you have to be a verbal street fighter or become part of the masses. People are looking for someone to tell them how to live.

Ignorance is easy to ridicule, but people who boast about who they were or what they had are even easier targets because they're hungry — and most hunger never goes away. It's the only thing they have to sustain them. They are even easier targets because the feeling usually increases over time. In any endeavor, whoever is the hungriest usually ends up winning. People become more dangerous when they're convinced that they are playing all the right notes. It doesn't even have to be in the right order for people to start listening; it only has to be consistent for the listener. Just because a person is heard doesn't mean that they're being listened to.

People have to be persuaded before they can be convinced. They also have to be convinced before they can be moved. Whoever is in control of the arts also controls the minds of others. There is a critical element to nearly everything, especially when it comes to human interaction. Successful people want to be right about everything. When the civility of a society is being destroyed, people must be made aware before it can be corrected.

# CHAPTER 18
# A REACTIONARY SOCIETY

W e're living in a time of uncertainty when people no longer need the truth in order to confirm whether something is or is not. To truly know any specific thing, you must know its relation to other things. How do we distinguish between the events that happen in our minds and those that happen in the world of physical objects? For example, the sun rises in the east and sets in the west and the sky is blue. Therefore, all skies are blue. The premises are true but the conclusion is false. The argument is therefore invalid.

It's a very compelling analysis when Aristotelian logic is applied. Naturalistic observation means we take part in what we are observing in order to learn what it is that we're observing. The voice of loyal opposition starts with one human looking over the horizon. Nearly every person of normal physical abilities can make observations. However, deductive argument is essential when making conclusions.

People have always had difficulty ascertaining the constant movement of things that are around them—it's in the nature of mankind. Everything is in a state of perpetual change; the sun goes up and down; the Earth is spinning; trees sway with the wind in one direction or another. More importantly though, people act to the change of their environment. It is believed that people are rational beings whose behavior is determined largely by their perceptions and choices. If that's true, then every individual's world is basically what their mind has made of it. That also means that human behavior is determined by environmental influences.

We're constantly stepping on a plane while traveling, uncertain of what's next. Perception is a creative process and no two people's perceptions are exactly the same. In a sense, we create our own world.

The skills that we carry can sometimes be astounding, because they can focus momentarily on the desires and needs of someone else. You can turn those same wants and needs to your own advantage. People first must understand that their thinking has been completely distorted by what they've seen and heard. This must first be made clear because trying to reason with someone who can't think along rational lines is always futile. In war, truth will be the first casualty. That is why there must be reassurance to the individual who's being made aware.

Remember, no man is an island, which means we're all part of something bigger than ourselves. There comes a time in everyone's life where they may walk over hot coals even when they don't have to, if for no other reason than to get out of their own way. Nothing is as permanent as change. The problem with change is nobody wants it until their lives have been made uncomfortable, and even then, people remain lazy. Remember that no revolution ever happened while the people we're fat and happy. That's why it's so important for people to be made aware of their environment and the circumstances before they can be moved.

There has to be a great incentive, otherwise all effort will be ineffective. They must understand that the rules of a normal functional society have been broken, and a reactionary society must respond accordingly. A strange thing happens when a person realizes that they've been lying to themselves about their own environment and remember truth is stranger than fiction. When a person suddenly realizes they've been wrapped in a web of deceit, they immediately want to untangle it first by telling another person about it. That's the way of all mankind. We are all natural busy bodies who want to let everything out, which sometimes can be a good thing. For example, if you know a part of society is being poisoned by what they are consuming, no sane person would want to chase down and embrace the same poison that's made the rest of society sick.

The fact of the matter is that the average person does not really care what's happening until they know that it's affecting them—period! That is the whole point. Until the windows of perception are cleansed, the only change will be more of the same. No rational, logical, sane person would argue that point. So, when an ill wind is blowing in, we know it but we can't see it. But we see the effect it's having—we hear it and can feel it; it's tearing down everything around us. No sensible person would not want to protect themselves from the elements of destruction.

The same concept should apply to our social environment. Would it be reasonable to sit in silence and do nothing and only hope for the winds of change? Would that be the civilized or the rational thing to do? Or should the people rise from the ashes and rubble that's been torn from a once great society?

A picture is worth a thousand words, so a visual representation of an idea has the power to impact the way people feel, think, and act. It gives people direction to where they want to go. Then, with consequential thinking, they start admitting and accepting what they need to do and where to go. When you realize that you've been allowing life to make your decisions, you also realize that you've been selling yourself short. That means visual representation will determine how people lead their daily lives. There is no easy solution that will be effective. This is because our society has a weak underbelly that walks in lockstep.

They've become so pernicious they don't believe in representation. That's why people have to be made aware through a visual image called mind mapping. It means that the problem has been identified by the onlookers or hearers. Now the solution is the image that will be projected through a display of emotional oratory the listener can identify with. This is the onset for mapping a solution. You cannot convince certain people of the truth simply because they are incapable of thinking. That means when world events are spinning in the opposite direction, you can't put all of your demands on the table initially.

Never try and outsmart your common sense. Nobody comes to the bargaining table at gunpoint. There comes a time when you have to ask yourself: Do you want to be right or do you want to be smart? When people demand to know the truth, they will eventually come to the source. Remember our senses often deceive us, thus we tend to see things as they appear.

World appearance is not the knowledge we can rely on. It is only a source of belief that is often false. It carries with it an immense influence that only fuels tolerance. That is why complexities are manufactured and not just born into existence. However, when we're complicit in exposing and understanding what has been done, it's not complex to anyone anymore. It's become evident that people are not really in tune with what's happening.

Man by nature is lazy and wants a society without opposition. That means a perfectly planned society is not built one step a time. More now than ever, people are really animalistic in their beliefs and likes. It is the New Age philosophy they've adopted that's become the normal way of life. The more that tolerance and diversity is insisted upon, the further we'll fall. A perfectly planned society will never happen as long as this continues. It's a pathway for the 'have-nots' to leech off of the rest of us.

Never forget, the stench starts at the top, and the street rats underneath will continue to do the bidding for a few pieces of silver. Hatred is a unifying agent and it's the secretion of the frustrated mind. Sensationalism is its motivator and self-advertisement is its result. The same ones who demand diversity are the very ones who take a wrecking ball to our Republic. It's a simple fact that if you love something, you don't want to transform it into something else. You would preserve and embrace it. I'm very consistent in my opinion, so if you're under the spurious notion that people aren't capable of getting enough of something, you're dead wrong.

Anytime you corner an animal it will strike back, and mankind has not transcended the zoological order. Therefore we have a defense mechanism that's part of our DNA. Social experimentation alone is the bacteria that's making the population sick. It's as aggressive as any cancer that attacks the body. Unlike the cancer that can be systematically removed, social tolerance must be completely eradicated all at once. If the rotten apples are not weeded out, the entire bunch will go bad. For the most part, people need to be angered in order to be moved. They also must know that the reward lies in the victory they will achieve. Always allow your participants to feel the emotional bond that is equal to none and they will follow with greater loyalty. Remember that all warfare is based upon deception.

You have to know your opposition and what they are capable of. Anytime you're left with an opportunity, always take full advantage of it. Sand in the glass falls quickly, so time is of the essence. In the absence of knowledge, you have to fill it with what you have. The pieces of the puzzle will eventually fall into place. Our fundamental principles have been violated, so do not rely on abstract principles for a solution. In many instances realism is cynicism, so the principles you follow will be problematic. Allowing something to metastasize before you act on it can be a positive step. The reason can be quite irrational, so logic has to fit into place.

You only will foster your own defeat by trying to achieve the impossible. That's why logic is so important. When people freely extol virtues that do not exist, it only helps to confuse a population that's been brainwashed beforehand. That means that the less we associate, the more we improve in our struggle for functioning participatory principles. The degradation of the human mind can be swift. So to provide this service to the Republic is of utmost importance. It must be the embodiment of a moral law that has been lost.

Our homeland is under attack by the very ones who scream social justice. Appeasement has only increased the aggressors' appetite. Things have faded into the gray, so much so that the once good people are few. The rest don't really care until it's too late. It is those who don't know history that haven't a clue where they are going simply because they don't know where we've been. So who do you want to run society? Who do you want at the helm?

The undesirables have become the enemy of the people and we are the people. There can be no dichotomy between right and wrong. Therefore the time is now for taking back what's been stolen. An already morally bankrupt nation can't afford to pay the price for something held hostage. That means when a resistance is led, the high cost of morality must come down. We are living in a time when the people are marginally attached to few principles we once held. They've been completely debased while nature abhors a vacuum. When we resist and push back, it will add additional layers of emotion for the resistance. In fact, it will create more space for our difficult experience. However clever this may be, it will not reduce the problem.

It will increase rapidly in the early stages. The art of handling the masses is a systemic process that requires energy. The struggle implies that we acknowledge what's happening among us. It also reminds us that something must be broken down in order to be identified. Once you look at the problem fully, it can then be broken down into manageable parts to better formulate an action plan.

If you want to solve a problem, you first get to the bottom of it. That means finding and eliminating the cause. There is no reasonable alternative that will bring a constructive solution. The courage we find will not be the absence of fear, it will be the conquest of it. Things are only easy when you have no preference, largely because it requires no courage at all. A driving force will bring victory for those who believe in it the most. In the final analysis, society will be better for the reconstruction that it requires.

# CHAPTER 19

# COMMUNICATION

Indeed, we are living in dangerous times, we have now however reached a new crescendo. The law has been stolen, while academia, media and dialogue have also been seized. The last thing to be stolen will be your freedom. There's a gulf between the law and justice. The law is not designed to seek out the truth. The security apparatus of our nation is under attack by civil liberty laws that are weaponized to weaken resolve against real issues. In the final conclusion, our passion must be to assemble and address any issues.

A warrior is someone who faces conflict and is willing to take lives so that others may live. That means there has to be awareness and relentless effort. When a state goes into decadence and decline, you get an equal opposite reaction. There is a seismic shift happening now and it's reached a new critical mass. This is a result of ultra-liberalism. We're living in a time of civil conflict. We've slipped as a civilization into the tolerance movement so much that we've been debased as human beings. This is why anger is the salvation for a nation that's being ripped apart.

Humanity always seems to accomplish a step up every thousand years. That time has come once again. That means that we change not only the substance but also the tenor of our course. Logic and reason have slowly been abandoned.

All science is built on objectivity, according to a set of logical and objective standards based on facts. Reason is a form of thinking that was developed by the ancient Greeks. A person can be faithful to something, yet be reasonable at the same time. Without objective reasoning, there would be nowhere for anyone to go.

Western civilization was built on objective reasoning. When everything is subjective you're only operating on how you feel. Logic and scientific methods create a more orderly world. Every living person wants the fruit that nature has to offer, there's no question about it. However, when the merit of the cause is perceived, it helps to create and shape events by bringing awareness. The people will then change social perceptions that will persuade them to think differently. Propaganda will never be an exact science because it deals with humans. We do however, know how it operates. You must treat the mind as an individual machine in order to create conviction among individuals.

Surviving is deeply implanted in every being on the plant. Surviving is also the challenge that nature imposes, therefore it's a challenge to stay alive. When taking a closer look, you see there's no purpose in life without challenges. There is an answer for everything after it's analyzed. Every person wants something more or better. No one wants what's rightfully theirs to be taken by another person, especially when it pertains to their survival or wellbeing. After people are made aware of their situation and what's happening to them, their survival mode becomes activated.

Every person possesses this trait; it's built into their DNA from the beginning. There's not an animal on the planet that refuses to fight for survival. As humans we are no different, only as humans, our thoughts go from words to deeds. In a crowd, every act is contagious. Then crowd interest will preside over one's own personal interest. Science does not guarantee peace and happiness. This is especially true when the moral forces have lost their strength and the old pillars of society are crumbling.

Civilized individuals will become less civilized when it is necessary. Cause and effect will then come naturally. It becomes necessary for the renewal of a civilization in order to bring prosperity back. Clear reasoning is the examination of evidence from the past. An unexamined life is not worth living because the individual has no purpose. They're simply existing without reason to exist.

Honor and loyalty work in conjunction. It's hard to truly have one without the other. When the two become connected you've established reason with a purpose. You now exist for something other than simply existing to say you're human. Tolerance is the last virtue that a dying society holds onto, and diversity always demands tolerance for those whom it seeks to destroy. When it becomes their sacred duty to take back a nation, it's because that nation has been stolen from its people.

# CHAPTER 20
# ASSERTIVENESS

We have become a society of assertive people and most everyone needs to have an adversary of some sort. Without an adversary, life for many people becomes boring, because almost everyone wants to have their own monologue of some kind. Mankind has learned over the years that the basic tool for manipulation of reality is the manipulation of words. It's common for people to want to look down with a critical eye from a high vantage point and shout out the problem. By doing so, people often overly involve themselves in social circles.

It's usually only when people finally withdraw because they want to be withdrawn, and are subjective because they want to generalize things by categorizing a whole group of people with an arrangement that appeals to them. Often by doing so, we exhibit our bias and expose a status quo. Most people will start to abhor anyone with a critical outlook on life. It's not plausible to categorize people, stereotype them, and expect everyone to submit just because we see symbolism in things. There is a generation gap that will determine how offended people will be, and as people, we have to think rationally and know where our survival lies.

We have become a nation of bombastic people to such an extent that we rarely slow down to realize that art imitates life and we can't even see it happening. So many times in life our cup runs over and we're too emotionally involved in our own social outlook that we allow ourselves to become blinded to the pertinent facts of what reality is or has become. It's easy to tell people that they're wrong. However the real task is to put those same people in possession of the truth. In doing so, we often find where our own strength lies.

Character can only be developed through our trials and suffering. It's only then that our vision is clear and our ambition inspired. We live in an age where we are drowning in a sea of information like the world has never seen. Yet more than ever, people are starving for wisdom. There always seems to be someone who claims to have the answer to the problem but lacks the moral courage to step up, so they invent their own moral philosophy to justify themselves.

> *"If you would persuade, you must appeal to interest rather than intellect."*
>
> —Benjamin Franklin

# CHAPTER 21

# SITUATIONAL AWARENESS

People want you to see the world through their twisted eyes. Never allow yourself to be deceived by their insanity. Instead, you meet them with a presentation of facts called stark reality. First, people should be made aware that their world has been left unfinished. When you look at the human landscape, you can see a breakdown of civilization. You're actually looking at components that are divided into parts. If you can market and sell this picture in the eyes of the beholder, everything will no longer be subjective to them. The objective reality comes into focus. It's also the same reason you cannot sell the exact concept to the same crowd later on. There has to be a continual addition to the message being given. Changes always have to be made to improve your argument.

It's a classic example of how to artfully sway the masses through awareness. It can also serve as a reminder that classical art is used to teach external lessons. External lessons help to change the opinion of others and exert influence especially when eloquence is properly applied. People are mostly a product of their own thoughts, or what they think they will become. Now they exist and their thoughts go to words and words go to action or deeds. When you create a theater of involvement, you also have to give a dramatic presentation based on current events.

When people are shocked, upset, or in a state of panic, they want to embrace social change. This is why the existing problem must be made evident then put on display for the eyes and the ears of onlookers. Remember, the theater of the mind is an outlet for rage. With this awareness, you must bring an illustrious display under a symbol to inform the listeners the world has been left unfinished.

We have evolved into a social atmosphere where it's easy and acceptable to categorize people. There's a hidden factor in just about everything. Whether it's good or bad, there's always something going on behind the scenes that we're unaware of. It's easy to categorize people but it's not easy to categorize reality until we walk the streets of reality. Nobody is immune to the ways of the world. We operate under a system where compromise has become the norm rather than the exception. Therefore, through a cumulative effort we allow ourselves to be put into our own psychological noose.

The mind can be the greatest destructive force or the greatest healing force in our life. It doesn't matter if something is or isn't psychosomatic. What matters is if it works or not. We have to realize that one side of an equation can always cancel out the other side. Once people realize that they're living in a totally brainwashed and controlled society, we can't very well blame them for taking advantage of a system. We should blame the system for letting the people take advantage of it. When we think about the stress we have, we should first think about what we would replace it with if we didn't have it. Anything we can't let go of, we don't own—it owns us. At some point we have to make a decision as to who we are. Because at some point, the end of the road waits for us all. Every person has to have belief and faith in something.

Faith is not a reasonable thing to have, nor is the lack of faith reasonable. Big chances always start in the most unlikely places with the smallest group of unlikely people. Human beings are unique in having the ability to learn from the experience of other people. They are also unique in their apparent disinclination to do so. In the final analysis, there is no perfection, so we live in a broken world and that doesn't give us an alibi for anything. So, in response, we rise to that occasion no matter the circumstances.

# CHAPTER 22
# SUBVERTING THE OUTRAGE

When you create something, you first have to imagine what it is before it's brought into being. In order to change and create the mind of the listener, you first have to establish communication. When you communicate you send out information by words and signals. Then with the power of language and tone, you can develop an elaborate structure with a concept. The image can easily be made symbolic by turning theory into reality and then putting it into practice.

Subtlety and precision will assist a message in being more effective. It will add potency while stimulating the senses and better influence the mind of the listeners. People typically overweight, channel their negativism in one direction or another, so they're usually swayed with little effort. This is also true because people always want something new or better so they can add to their lives whenever possible. This is how the orator calculates the weakness of onlookers and takes advantage of an opportunity. There has to be something offered for one to consider another's wishes. Therefore, when acting on behalf of the people in the interest of public consumption, it's sometimes necessary to speak one's mind without restraint.

A parasite is an organism that lives off another living organism, depriving it of its nutrients. It usually exhibits its presence by causing damage or death to its host. It must be known by all and maintained at the community's expense that freeloading social parasites are cut from society's flesh. This service will be for those concerned for justice, wellbeing, progress, and eventually peace. The object in focus is a functional requisite, and that is a societal need. If a societal need is not met, damage and eventually death will occur.

Now that we can see at least some of that need, how do you start the process of supplying that need? There is an answer to everything and in this instance it's a call to action through effective intervention. Everyone wants to have their place at the table, whether they admit it or not. The revenge people often seek is always best when served cold. The most effective way to rid the unwanted or defeat an enemy is to cut off the supply line and isolate all subjects. The act or process for obtaining an answer for something is its end purpose.

There is a moral outrage that's turning into a societal nightmare and this is why an answer has to be given. First you have to unify the weak for proper assembly with a purpose and reason. They don't have to understand the reason, they only have to know what the reason is. Brains are like muscles. You have to remember and keep in mind that all actions and events require people to be present. There is no debating this point. You can't expect something to happen unless a fuse has been lit. Lighting a simple fuse may only require one person, but its preparation takes the combined effort of universal physical, emotional, and mental resources.

When countdown commences, the action must be taken before the time diminishes or else all effort will be futile. That brings back the question of what that action includes. Subverting the will of the people is mind over matter. As insidious as it may sound, it's sometimes necessary to subvert people's will in order to do what's right for their own wellbeing. Once people believe and know that their actions are morally justified, they won't mind nearly as much when the time comes for change.

When a wound is inflicted on an enemy, it sends a shock wave to the nerve center. It's an experience that lets the recipient know that it's an unwanted presence. The wars of the past help us to more easily define wars of the present, and with that said, people are always more receptive to a concept or idea after a small taste of victory is achieved. There are no easy solutions to complex problems. That makes it necessary sometimes for a free-spoken individual to speak unrestrained. It then may be a matter of conjecture if a decision is acted upon.

Freedom is having the right to point out what's happening, question it, and watch it catch fire among the people. This is especially important in an age of such lies and chicanery. From time to time, societies through the ages have allowed themselves to travel so far up river that they are unable to find their way back. They are so far into their own world of make believe that they're no longer able to recognize what's real and what's not.

Nearly 2,500 years ago, Plato wrote, "The average man rarely sees the actors, only the shadows on the cave wall." People have become so accustomed to defending what they knew to be wrong, they can no longer tell what's true and what's not. When you tell yourself the same lie over and over, it eventually becomes what you think is true. Brutus conspired to assassinate Caesar, then later defended his action to do so. It's the same now, except today, an entire way of life is being assassinated from the inside out.

There has to be something in the mind's eye in order to reflect or hope for change to occur. The basic principle of chemistry is mathematics. When you break something down with chemistry, you can know for sure what it is you have. When you can identify what you have and bring it out in the open, you're more able to dominate it exquisitely. Things will then become so balanced for the spectator that the exactness of the observation will change the opinion of the skeptics. This will have a far-reaching effect and the people will no longer have such pity for the vermin.

Many will act brutally and become remorseless, especially when the facts become evident. The exchange theory advocates that behavior of people, particularly in social organizations, are motivated by expectations in return for their participation or loyalty to a cause. An accurate analysis of human behavior can best be learned from these same participants based on the amount of wealth and privilege they've been afforded.

# CHAPTER 23
# FACING THE EPIDEMIC

Society is being ripped apart, and the people who are watching it happen are going to have to make a decision. We're living through a cultural madness—a mass hysteria with no limits. When you lose the right to criticize, things become very dangerous because you lose the concept of a free society. This is where I'll be part of your mental geography and explain. We're on a downward spiral because the subject matter has to be important to some. It's the non-innovative people that are stifling civilization by running dialogue and affecting society as a whole. When we lose the right to criticize, we lose everything.

The people who are driving this are intellectually deficient and ignorant of history. If you can't understand what is right or wrong, there's no way to bring a purer or better society. The self-satisfied don't even know they're digging their own grave by admitting no reality other than their own. In actual reality, they're all suffering from a mental complaint that has no basis or foundation. This simply needs to be kicked in by those who are being silenced. This is what brought down the Roman Empire and it poses the same threat today. In other words, it's just as dangerous now as it was then, only now it's on a much larger scale.

This time it's turning into a global epidemic where everyone loses, not just the Romans. If this goes unchecked, everyone will go down with the Titanic, only this time there are no lifeboats. No one called for help because everyone has been silenced. Remember, writer Martin Niemöller said, "First they came for the Jews and I said nothing, I wasn't a Jew. Then they came for the gypsies and other undesirables, I said nothing, I wasn't a gypsy. Then they came for the communist and trade unionist, I said nothing because I was neither. When they finally came for me, there was no one left to say anything." Any way you choose to analyze what's happening, it brings a gloomy prospect.

Whenever a nation allows itself to be overcome because its citizens have been brainwashed into thinking that offending someone is criminal in nature, it's lost its defense. Anyone who chooses to take on a Biblical prospective on this can go to Isaiah 1:7; "Your country is desolate, your cities are burned with fire. Your land strangers devour in your presence, and now it is desolate as overthrown by strangers." Now, if you believe that then you must know what diversity and tolerance can and will bring. So, where do we go from here?

Do we just wait and see how bad things may get? It's much easier to eradicate harmful bacteria before it spreads. When you find a cancer, you cut it out and hope you catch it all before it's too late. Why would you not do the same when something harmful enters your homeland? At some point, there needs to be a lesson remembered, and remind ourselves what's past is prologue. If no one makes an observation or takes measure of our existing position, they'll be no way to know where we are in the world. Knowing there's a problem and identifying it will take you one step closer to the solution.

That is about as far most people in the world are willing to go. They all want to continue eating at the table but none want to help in the kitchen. An enabler allows or makes it possible for a person or thing to do something. Therefore, you're helping a problem exist by not being a part of the solution. There's an answer to everything, which means that when you reply with words or action, you've responded in some way. Doing nothing by ignoring the strain it imposes will further the ability of a destructionist and ultimately lead to the ruin of society. We either allow ourselves to be ruled over tyrannically, where everyone gets fleeced, or we prevent activity with an opposing faction.

# CHAPTER 24
# THE LEADING PRINCIPLE

Everything starts with an idea: a mental image that can rise independently of sense perception. The mind impresses its forms of sensibility on the original data of the senses. It then orders them according to the categories of thought. An idea typically goes from words to deeds; how fast depends on the person. By hammering a person's character, they are more susceptible, affected, and formed by external influence.

People who are vulnerable are easily swayed. Their thoughts become malleable and their shape can be changed permanently, usually through the application of stress. However, nothing is as permanent as change. You have to recognize what's hostile before your mind interferes with a concept or idea. It's easy to create your own crisis whether it is internal or external.

When you become addicted to your own propaganda, you create a crisis on both ends of the spectrum. In order to revert back to the standards you once held in esteem, you have to acknowledge the direction of your thoughts. That in itself will be the highpoint in your moral and cultural activity. The equivalent of a crisis is a difficult opportunity. You can eventually get an opportunity out of a difficulty in most instances. The problem being that as opportunities arise, we often grasp for them without considering a principle or a plan. With that being the case, you constantly have to make adjustments with each new occurrence.

Society, the proletariat, and the court of public opinion are already suspicious. The more refined you become, the more vulnerable you may become. All living things most consume other living things—it's the way of all flesh. That's why free thinkers are dangerous to all power structures. Rome did not pass away peacefully, it was assassinated.

The mind does not exist by itself. The world was here before we moved in. When you start tugging at nature and interrupt the natural order of things, you soon find out that you need nature to survive but it doesn't need you. People need to know where their boundaries lie and when their safety is at stake.

Mythology is often something we need to gain a better prospective. Looking back on Greek mythology, Daedalus, while in prison, built the wings for his son Icarus. The wax held the wings' feathers in place. He then told Icarus, "Do not fly too close to the sun or the wax will melt." The boy eventually flew too close to the sun and crashed into the sea. All too often we make the same mistake.

We want to enjoy the comfort of our own opinion without the discomfort of thought. None of us have ever really absolved the need to perfect our own opinion. While thinking that we're infallible, we quickly go from words to deeds without a second thought, even when our own safety is hanging in the balance. There's no time to understand what that something is. The minute that you are caught in a logical flaw and jump to another argument, it only makes you counterproductive. There can be no learning curve. How can the orator grant understanding if no logical disposition is being given?

Only through powerful exhortation can the minds and hearts of the hearers be easily persuaded, whatever the incentive. It always has to be appealing and pleasing to the senses in some way. This is made possible by rendering and making visible a chief talking point. Never exposing what could be detrimental is imperative and equally important.

The future of the individual or any social group is not necessarily predetermined in every instance. Fate sometimes has a way of stepping in and playing the hand that you would least expect. Never think that anyone is guaranteed full control of the ship and its destination.

It's a perilous misconception to think that by chartering your own course you'll hit the exact spot you seek. Not only is that highly improbable, but more often than not, you get the exact opposite. You have to take into account that societies go through fads and have lost their connection to logic and what's realistic. With that brings all the more reason for the orator to demand the suppression of human feeling.

# CHAPTER 25
# SOCIAL ENGINEERING MOVING FORWARD

Progress in any movement requires greater attention to detail. That means people are finally waking up to realize what's happening and admitting it. Then you can effectively reshape public opinion. The message has to be substantive. Remember that most of the social outcasts are the ones telling other people how to act, yet are leading miserable lives themselves. They think freedom solely consists of telling others what they can and cannot do. The biggest problem with that is there's little opposition or resistance on the other side. They are simply lying down or forgetting how to resist. Man by nature is inherently lazy.

That also means that strength for support must come in numbers. No man is an island. That also means we have to go from one to many moving forward. For this to happen there must be complete exposure of the vermin that are wreaking havoc in modern day society. The people have been deprived of the truth. When the truth does occasionally come out it's instantly sanitized by the left-wing faction. Now we must point out who has polluted our nation and poisoned the mind of our youth. We must hold these truths to be self-evident in what we call a free and open society. If that is the case, let freedom ring out in this republic and never presume to know for whom the bell tolls.

It tolls for the people who have now been awakened to the truth. We are now in the course of human events where it has become necessary to separate the ties that bind us. So, let us separate from the saboteurs by kicking in the filth that's contaminating the people's republic. The great society has been eviscerated and must be rebuilt to its proper form.

You can't reason with the lie that's being insisted upon, the logic simply will not fit into place. A good defense requires a good offense, which does not mean taking a shortcut to lessen the odds of defeat. More times than not, a shortcut makes you come up short.

We have to offer up our best, a thin disguise doesn't change a thing. Logic is a superpower that brings things into prospective and without it you defy reason. The nature of human thought is asking questions and trying to answer them within the realm of reality, and not just relying on your own beliefs. Interpretation of facts is largely based on a person's beliefs. What you believe is usually based on what you are used to hearing on a daily basis. When you connect the two, it can make an immoral act seem moral. This is proven true when the evidence of learning is the outcome. Cause and effect are more evident when the facts are made known.

There's a storm raging on the home front and most people do not even realize it. The polluted mind and psychology of this nation have gotten out of control. Super logic says to make way for the ones that matter. Allowing infectious insanity to spread among us only topples progress. Instead of losing sight of what's real, we have to take time to realize what's happening and the potential ramifications. That also means if you don't like what's happening, you have the option to propose a viable solution and come forward. This is especially true when an inferior portion of society is indecent to the rest and therefore not favorable to anyone else.

Instead, we have widespread interference or flat-out denial, which is a shorthand term for a wide range of psychological defenses propped up by the liberal left. This is done to protect themselves from a realization of facts. These defensive maneuvers, all of which distort reality, can appear in many different forms. One would be minimizing a problem — admitting we have a problem but making it sound as if it is not a concern, when in reality, it is. For example, saying we only have a small percentage of the population out of control, when it's really much bigger.

The second would be rationalizing by offering alibis to justify what the vermin are doing. The third is intellectualizing by avoiding emotions and personal awareness and dealing only on the level of generalization, analysis, or theorizing. The fourth is diversion by changing the subject to another subject in order to avoid a topic that might appear to be threatening. The fifth comes right before hostility starts and that's blaming the rest of society for what happened to them in the past, which is a direct result of their behavior but placing the responsibility on us. The last is becoming more angry and violent whenever a reference is made to the conduct of the entire race.

The primary function of this behavior is to protect an entire race from the realization that he or she is inferior to all others and dependent on everyone else while tearing a nation apart at the seams. With time, they become more and more dependent, thereby developing more needs. This creates adverse effects over time and also creates more conflict. This is why we have to relentlessly impose awareness of reality. We can't allow knowledge to be blocked while the rest of society is being threatened by savage beasts. It's like mixing together the pieces of two puzzles when one-half doesn't fit with the other.

We have to change course and steer the ship or we'll all go down with it if this continues. The same ones who are enemies of rationality have become the disrupters of cooperative social relations. This is why we must learn to trust the journey even if we don't understand it. In order to embrace change, we must introduce increased awareness and clarity into the nature of our conflict. When people have more insight, they are more willing to take action. The anger we bear is often conceptualized as arising from either fear or pain. That in turn puts us on the precipice of a new era. Remember that the emotions people have guide their perceptions of the world.

There's an answer for everything, so never think there's not a solution for the unreasonable plunder, destruction, and seizure of a nation. First, you have to take time to know that we've been poisoned. Then understand that the same ones who are spreading the poison have an agenda, usually finding common ground and pointing fingers. They put everyone else on their current piety and prospective. It only serves to overshadow the real story. This all becomes clear when people untwist their thinking and learn to navigate their new-found reality.

Valued highly in our society is being comfortable, so the pursuit of discomfort for the sake of what we recover is vital. Learning this can be a cruel lesson because it will give the test first and the lesson later. The rallying cry is an instrument to be used and not a deity to be worshiped. This is especially true when human parasites with an illness are multiplying in epic proportions.

Control is an organizing force and a nation's spirit is worth more than the freedom of spirit. Sacrifices have to be made for the good of mankind. Instead, we have an unfriendly part of society who would vote to take property away from the ones who have earned it if they we're allowed. This is why the split of individuality must preside in the homeland.

Trying something new to combat a problem is not necessarily the answer. Instead we should try what's proven to work. The only solution is to separate the productive from the non-productive, then eliminate the non-productive. Our struggle for the new mankind will then pierce through difficult choices that have to be made to achieve the greater good of mankind.

Diversity is nothing more than a code word for tearing society apart. It's used as a mouthpiece for the collective unconscious. We no longer see the greatness of a nation, we're only seeing the tolerance of a nation. The majority has been tricked into thinking that there's no lost civility in a demographic society. Our society has been polluted with the vile imagery that's being propagated by the watered-down and weakened standards. The poison that's seeping into society at large continues to work a broken system. Yet, the same lies are told over and over to make people believe that it's true. It's a successful strategy that's been used on man since the beginning of time. Make no mistake about it, it's because of this that people have no warrior spirit.

People have lost the will to fight back; they've simply become passive. If a nation loses the ability to know the reality of the world, it's lost the ability to purge itself of its enemies. There's not an animal in the world that refuses to defend itself. We have a population that is confusing what's popular with what's futile. It's become a useful tool for the ones who are propping up left-wing ideology. It has to be known that people are more inclined to follow a person than a policy. Logic and scientific method teach people how to reach a conclusion on a subject so they can think differently about a society.

When a person of strong will becomes filled with honor and feels duty bound, they are able to speak the power of truth. This is essential in a time of crisis, especially when a futile but popular uprising becomes an issue. We have to look at the complete picture. We will cease to have a nation unless the people awaken. Every person has a defense mechanism. It's built into the DNA of every human. When we're overly passive, we subdue this mechanism and we become an antithesis to the human spirit. We become more inclined to tolerate the immoral decay of society.

# CHAPTER 26

# I THINK, THEREFORE I AM

People who are not known for their logic are known only for their emotion. It's nearly impossible to reason with someone who is locked into a belief. People are so locked into what they've heard for so long, they are too ashamed to admit what they know to be true. In their own mind, they distort reality. The best way to change someone's mind about something is to give them hope. Most people don't want to change what they have until they're given some kind of hope for something better.

Change is nearly always inconvenient, but progress is impossible without it. Since the beginning of the human race, people have been looking to fulfill themselves with something better. Mankind didn't learn to just start emptying his or her soul. Every society has looked for something to relieve the pain of their environment. Everyone is in some way looking to get away from the variations of existence. They want a way out of their daily lives, without giving up anything. No animal in the world would want to be weaker in the jungle. The same goes for humans, because nobody in their right mind would want to put themselves at a disadvantage by weakening themselves.

It is necessary to look at the totality of the picture instead of the linear view. Instead of blaming everything on the circumstances, people have forgotten how to go out and create the circumstances they yearn for. Some people have greatness foisted upon them and some people have to find it on their own. But to everything there is a cycle. There is a beginning, a middle, and an end. Even the worst reaction we have to something has to have an end.

There's nothing that a human can make that another human can't break. There's also nothing we can break that someone else can't put back together again.

Miserable ideas, in most cases, have to be taught. Information and communication are often used in the same sentence, but they signify two different things. Information is something that can be obtained. Communication is absorbing the information that we receive. It's impossible to communicate with certain people because no one can appeal to them. Nobody can change the mind of someone who has no mind. There's nothing that one person can say to another that can't be misinterpreted in one way or another.

People want to be in an advantageous position in their own way. By nature they put forth more effort to harm others rather than help themselves. The logic doesn't follow the social strata. Yet, there is always something appealing in saying what we think everyone else may be thinking. We are living in a cultural decline where far too many people think of themselves as a victim. They usually think they are justified and well within their rights. In reality, there is no one who does not represent some type of threat to someone or something, somewhere in the world.

# CHAPTER 27
# THE WORLD ACCORDING TO US

W e're living in an age of lies and fabrication based on rumor and innuendo. Everyone is in their own personal agony, whether they choose to admit it or not. We live in the human condition. Chasing after happiness is what drives people relentlessly and sometimes mad.

Each individual feels religion is a narcissistic thing that's necessary at the end of the day. Anything we find useful and inexpensive will always meet the most resistance. People by nature have a narcissistic view of the world instead of having a view according framed by reality. Our thoughts are controlled by our cerebral cortex. Without discernment or an open mind it's impossible to be realistic. The reason people don't want to face reality is simply because it most often doesn't feel good.

Courage is being able to do something that you are afraid to do. We have fears, and all too often we're intimidated. Some people overcome their fears, some don't. Whether or not it's sought after, there is an answer to everything. It's usually the people who live with and overcome their fears that end up being the best and the brightest.

The mind, unlike anything else, is the most vulnerable thing we have. It can be poisoned without any immediate symptoms or pain. People have become accustomed to dressing their image in a prevailing fashion. A good actor will stay on point and always find a way to deceive someone. A bad actor is unable to successfully market and sell what he's peddling. A con man has to have his confidence or he loses his ability to con. It's the most influential tool he can have for sculpting someone else's mindset.

The most effective people are ones who are more astute and biased than anyone else. Only a small percentage aspire to be the best at something by trying to improve or invent. The remaining percentage settles for what's left to be desired. Someone who's shrewd, quick and advantageous can easily lead and push other people to the next plateau. We cannot enter into and advance in a learning society without giving recognition to what's happening.

Only a small number offer selfless service by any measure to the good of the upcoming generation. An opportunist will always bring an obligation with an attached debt. We already have the opportunity to be creative with concepts and material. Instead of being self-sufficient, people become more dependent on someone or something. We only want to conserve the obvious necessities in our daily lives.

Civilization resides in the court of public opinion. Everyone wants to get somewhere easier, faster, and cheaper than before, giving little or no thought to a much broader spectrum. Ever since humans learned to mount something and ride it they've been fascinated with motion. We've evolved from riding camels to donkeys, boats, horses, bicycles, trains, cars, planes, helicopters, and moon rockets.

In 150 years, we have transcended the telegraph to the internet. Having unobstructed access to innovation is good if we have the desire to find out where it may lead. In the final analysis, no matter what we do or which direction we decide to take, there is no easy way out. We're still suffering from the vicissitudes of existence and trapped under the wheel of life.

# CHAPTER 28
# TO EVERYTHING IN LIFE THERE IS A CYCLE

People are naturally inclined to think that if they watch and listen to something or someone long enough they feel like they've become part of it. Human history is mostly the result of people looking out for themselves. People by and large want to seize all that is attainable. The history of mankind teaches us that the most productive force on earth is human selfishness. In any major event, there is an ulterior motive somewhere to be found. We live in repetition of our own views and interest.

The majority of all people are subjective toward themselves and objective toward others. In a consumer society, there are two kinds of people, the prisoners of addiction and the prisoners of envy. Self-actualization cannot be pursued, therefore we cannot construct life to make sense. People do not find themselves — they create themselves.

When you realize and know who you are and what you want to say you have achieved self-actualization. To everything in life there is a cycle. We live out one tragedy after another. An even keel is a short-lived evolution in the lives of most people. We're traveling over 17,000 miles-per-hour and never in a straight line, rather a constant movement of the up and down.

When suffering from poverty or misfortune, people are never satisfied or content with small gains. Even when it ceases, nobody's satisfied, they immediately want something more. Society has forgotten how to wait on something. Everyone wants it now, quick, and in a hurry. People no longer realize that they may need to suffer a little now to succeed later in life. The higher someone's reasoning, the higher the chances are for a break-down into reality. In many cases, it is better to lose a desire than to gain a possession.

The five stages of a grief cycle are: denial, anger, bargaining, depression, and acceptance. So, people start by substituting what they don't have with an acquired vice so they can play the victim. The masses are vastly uneducated. It's only emotion and hatred that controls them. They are the most mallea-ble of people. There's always someone leading the movement of theoretical interest with practical application. It's mostly the highly uninformed or uneducated that go into academia because their unable to do something on their own. They attempt to teach others to do what they can't do. Every-thing continues to run exactly on time no matter the circumstance.

It is a perpetual cycle of high and low and it's called reality. Belief and see-ing are often both wrong. People are never really moved by reaching a goal, because success is a stale finale. All the excitement is in the effort placed into achieving the goal.

In the mind of the average person, they are on the brink of an abyss anyway so there's a big market now for anyone who wants to trade in their unfortu-nate circumstances for a little safety and security. It becomes their one and only sustenance. At some point in everyone's life, they have to decide where they want to go for sustenance and reality. The malcontent usually have faith in something that's not compatible with reason. When a disaffected group are told they are being oppressed continually, they will eventually believe it and turn to someone who can market and make use of the issue.

Sympathy comes with a price for anyone who's willing to keep paying for it. If you negotiate, you must be able to navigate the diversity quotient, because it will always be there. When we're unable to navigate what we create, we set ourselves up for a hollow victory that comes at a great cost, but which is not a victory at all. The battle is won by depleting all energy and resources so we end up losing the war. Much like that of Pyrrhus (king of Epirus) over the Romans in 279 B.C. Resistance fatigue is the number one cause of defeat, especially when there's no architectural plan in place to move forward.

No matter what rallying cries the orators give the crowd, no matter what noble purpose is being preached, when people are told their being oppressed, it becomes a simple matter. It's no longer necessary to drag anyone in. No matter how resistant or fanatical a group may become, it will only increase as more are recruited. Any idea without power to move or act is inert and should not be received by the mind.

Submission is capitulation and more than anything, people are enslaved by their own desires. Words can be the most powerful weapon depending upon where they originate. Rage and anger motivates people and keeps them going. Language can be of great interest if we pay attention to it and no interest if we pay no attention to it.

In the final analysis, if we're studying something that we can define, we eventually end up with the truth. It's hard to know the truth until we study it. Instead, people have allowed their rational mind to be erased. Art imitates life, so we take in only what appeals to us and then immerse ourselves in it. Everything else is discarded before it can be studied or analyzed. In the end, if we do not engage in our ideas and we leave everything up to academia, we will crumble.

# CHAPTER 29
# SEDITION

We are a nation in decline with little regard for the reality in which we live. We have become people of conquest and it's a very dim place when we look through the dark glasses of reality. Our society has become void of values, partly because people have become brainwashed into thinking that tolerance is the finest of virtues. There is an appearance of impropriety among our nation that is all consuming and as a result, combativeness is emerging.

People demand entitlements more so now than ever. We live in a very porous social world where people all have a very keen analysis of one another. People can be quite marginal in some regard and in other ways they tend to give an overbearing comparison. It's common for someone to come across with an interesting quotient or an archetypical image because they are full of reprehensible neglect. It is for this reason that so many people have chosen to take a hardened position to the point that they are so full of bitterness that they take it out on others.

Sociopathic people are constantly suspicious of everyone around them and they lie to get their way because they're goal oriented. There is something that's always appealing to a disaffected group of people when someone tells them "Don't believe what you see, believe what I tell you to see." It's usually the person already on the side of the controlling faction who creates a paradigm with a keen intent.

It is the sociopathic liars who have people believe they're benign, caring, and trustworthy because they have social skills and manipulative ways. Sociopathic liars speak with a forked tongue that they've used their entire life. They lie incessantly in a garish manner, trying to encourage or influence a large demographic. Pathological liars lie because it feels good. Compulsive liars lie because it's a habit and they are addicted to lying at any given opportunity. In the final analysis, they are both conscious of what they do. Instability is bad for anyone else and good for them, so they capitalize on it in every way possible.

This is all done through the art of sedition. No normal person would want to lie and rule over everyone else all the time. Only a narcissistic, nihilistic extremist would find that appealing. These people are nearly always counterproductive in everything they say and do. This is the antithesis of a philosophy-based moral order that the intelligentsia propagate with their despotic mentality as they attempt to cleanse the last vestige of every caveat in our Republic.

I will conclude with this particular point. We have a sordid past, not just in this nation, but in every nation. Therefore, we now have division that has been magnified. When a new wind blows in, it changes the nature of everything. You don't have to be an astrophysicist to understand any of this. People have allowed their sense of reality to be destroyed and the people who have a little insight or self-awareness are few. It's the people who have a God-like complex who are some of the worst people on the planet. Anyone who has allowed themselves to think that the world is just as kind as they are is under a perilous misconception. History teaches us that there will come a time when we have to converse and ask what we have.

> *"No man is an island entire of itself, every man is a piece of the continent, a part of the main. If a clod be washed away by the sea, Europe is the less as well as if a promontory were, as well as if a manor of thy friends or of thine own were. Any*

*man's death diminishes me because I am involved in mankind and therefore never send to know for whom the bell tolls, it tolls for thee..."*

—John Donne

# CHAPTER 30
# DEFINING REASON

Fulfilling an objective often means suppressing human feelings. Preoccupied thoughts can be surmountable, but they often come at the expense of reason. While we feel something, it's because we've become aware through the senses. Sympathy is an emotion that can give someone conviction for something other than reason. That, in turn, will often lead to a weak response. It will make susceptibility all the more present.

The principle of reality is the reason for something. Knowledge is derived from reason, therefore, when you connect the two, you gain understanding. When you have the ability to solve a problem, you also need the ability to observe and respond appropriately. When you observe something you come to know it by what you're seeing. It is, however, important to take measure of an observation before an analysis is made. How we see and approach items will largely define who we are. Only by careful examination can you recognize and understand the poison woven into fabric that holds things in place. By public demonstration, people are easily made aware through their own observation of facts made obvious.

The backbone of any movement is the power of its people. The problem will be the people who stand in the way of the solution. They are the opposing factor that will attack with impunity. The way to counteract this in the early stages is by informing and alerting the population. People must first be put into a near state of fear or panic before they are willing to act on the solution to a problem. This is made possible by alerting the public to the fullest extent. All action at this point must be positively legal in order to advance and draw support. This is where cause and effect play an important role.

Now that people have been made aware that their livelihood is at stake and prosperity is under attack, you have their attention. When you have someone's attention, it means they're listening because it sounds important. Cause and effect can now be provided. What or who is causing the present threat and what effect will it have? This is the question asked by the people who are now listening.

The only reason people unite is because they have a common interest. They all come together because they either love or hate an idea. When that interest involves being deprived, having something taken, or having something owned, they all rally around it. They become like Indians beating a war drum and chanting around a fire as the white men came to steal their land.

Reason plays no factor whatsoever, the only concern is what happened, or what's about to happen and who's making it happen. For example, when a country declares war and sends its troops into battle, they don't explain why the enemy did what it did. Nobody really bothers to ask, and those who do rarely take time to understand anyway. The fact of the matter is that society is already suspicious, so anytime there's a revelation of any noticeable amount, it's instantly seized upon. Then they will dance around it and make noise until something new or better comes along.

Anytime people continue to take a myopic focus on a subject, they slowly lose sight of the real issue until they no longer realize what they're fighting against. This is why you give a verbal, then instinctive, point of view when handing over reason. To maintain effort among people, it takes continuous renewal of cause in order to keep persuasion and motivation afloat.

When people have a motive, it's because a need or desire has been detected by the senses. That is what prompts an individual to act because an occurrence has inspired them by alerting and conveying something to their senses. Anytime you assemble something, you're putting together pieces that are ready made to fit. Each piece is designed by the sculptor or artist who builds it. The same concept is applied to humans. All people created we're not meant to fit together in the same place at the same time—the pieces simply will not fit.

Honor does not live among thieves, nor does it want to. No functional society adapts and changes its mold for foreign objects that weren't meant to fit into that place—nor should it. When we ingest poison, our body's senses usually tell us that we've taken in something we shouldn't. The same is true for human survival. You have to identify the harmful poison when it lives among you, calling it by name. A small dose of strychnine can give you a wonderful high, but the tolerance increases over time. How much will you allow before it kills you?

# CHAPTER 31
# EXTOL THE VIRTUES
# OF THE PEOPLE

Life is fundamentally tragic but people are afraid to say that it is. It's like the swinging sands of time when someone finally does say it. We as a society have been given the facsimiles of advertisement. We're living in a time when we are constantly being told that everything is okay. When people are influenced by everything they see and hear every day, they forsake the very things that preserve their survival. Adversity often brings prosperity, but it can also bring out the worst in people. Everyone wants influence in the court of public opinion. Most people don't want to be the ones to disrupt the natural order of things; they only want to follow the trend.

We must always retain the right to be a critical supporter of what we believe in. Sometimes words fail us and we have to turn to something greater than ourselves. People have learned over time to utilize a problem by causing a reaction and making it bigger. It becomes necessary to illustrate a principle while we exaggerate much of what we omit. A society is only as free as its participants. There is a far deeper psychosis beneath the veneer of something we see as so simple. We all want to believe that there is power to positive thinking. It would be unpopular to say some people are born to do certain things and some people are just born.

An effective teacher has to say a lot of things that are not popular. The price of liberty is eternal vigilance. The day someone starts believing someone else shouldn't judge their character is the day they start believing in something superficial. Truth is the torch that gleams through the fog without dispelling it.

Everyone bears the stamp of their own condition. Our excessive tolerance is our own state of mind and we cannot condemn it without condemning ourselves. Life is like a ship on the ocean, it can be dangerous and we never know what we're going to encounter. When we know we're heading off course and straight into an iceberg, we can't just wait for someone to turn the rudder for us. The iceberg will start tearing away at the hull until there is nothing left.

# CHAPTER 32
# CYNICISM

**F**reedom is having the ability to manage our own lives. Our personal happiness depends on what our life is when we compare it with what we wanted it to be (Self-Actualization). Life can be like an ocean, the waves keep coming in. An ill wind blows in and we think all is lost and we can't go on. A person has to learn to navigate their way through life without doing harm to themselves. We're all quizzical to some degree. Some people refuse to change their sentiment simply because their brain is so rigid.

No person is born unto themselves. Every person is preceded by another person. If people are not controlled in their rapacious behavior, they will end up with nothing. The windows of reality have to be cleansed in order to see how bad things really are and see life as it is.

Daily exchanges of the mind are a good thing to have because people have made an art out of doing nothing and wrapping their own minds around it. No one should lie down and just let technology and prosperity roll over them just because they don't understand certain things in life. We are more often treacherous and vulnerable without calculation.

Human beings have a greater capacity to take things for granted more than any other creature on Earth. Everyone wants a reputation for generosity but they want it at the cheapest price. Everyone wants the feeling of being indigenous. Especially when they think they've found their place in the world they thought was mundane. We all have the tendency to be subversive to others to some extent, especially when our routine is somehow interrupted by someone.

Cynicism plays a part in everyone's life in one way or another—some more than others. People use cynicism as a crutch more often than not. It's the easy way out for lazy people because they don't have to try. When someone is cynical all the time, they no longer feel the need to be realistic about anything.

In order for technology to advance and prosperity to keep moving forward, reality must take precedence. Nature can't be fooled, no matter how hard we try.

> *"A fish always rots from the head down…"*
>
> —Unknown

# CHAPTER 33
# THE VOICE OF PARTY POLICY AND LOGICAL DISPUTATION

Before a conflict is put into action, you have to express and identify its true nature. Anything indicating a threat must be addressed with a specific and detailed description. You must display the full range and its potential effect. Only through logical thought and ultimate awareness will the mind arrive at absolute knowledge of the truth. With that, the mind will then be aware of itself.

The voice of party policy must speak a vernacular that will serve the entirety of the masses. First in this action of awareness, the mind will take an immediate grasp of the subject. Then, on further reflection, the primary subject will be opposed by contradictory evidence. Finally, when considering the multiplicity of evidence, the mind will arrive at a resolution. Throughout history this has been the process and development of political and social institutions, science, art, and religion.

Through dialectics, the opposite in opinion or apparent contradictions can be resolved with logical disagreement. A constant and unyielding wind is a driving force that will eventually affect the entire landscape and all its inhabitants. When giving an example, the necessity is to bring about and display meaning. This will show cause and all its purpose. A greater awareness will always be essential for expansion. The masses are mostly malleable. They naturally have self-loathing while trying to project it on society as a whole.

With proper handling of words to action, this can be used or channeled in another direction for a better purpose and cause. People want to willingly embrace a mutual security treaty in some form. They can't just allow their minds to be totally empty. They would just be left to wonder aimlessly without reason or self-identity. When a sense of freedom from uncertainty and self-consciousness begins to emerge, motivation or self-willed commitment will come into play for the people.

When reason comes into focus, people will know who and what to be and where they want to go. It is at this point that not only has communication been established but a point of contact with people. Now communication has to be maintained with constant continuity among party lines. This helps to keep an individual moving in a forward motion. You must remember when communicating with others, a thought may only introduce a possibility. But a thought also deals with the representation of reality as well. Without a voice of logical disputation, the eventual societal turmoil will be on the upward path.

# CHAPTER 34
# ASSEMBLING THE MASSES

**A** civilized society is favorable to the arts and sciences in a community with respect to its culture. When a society evolves over time, its culture slowly erodes due to the pollution of human activities. The social behavior of humans is a basic determination of how rapid the society declines.

A servant of civility is not to be confused with a civil servant. A servant of civility is concerned, closely associated, devoted to redeveloping and training the minds of others. Humans are social beings who are analytical and usually rational by nature. The social values of any society diminish as the multiculturalism and subcultural differences among its population are interwoven. This upsets the normal course of activities among people. There can be no egalitarian principle in any society expected to advance in its traditional beliefs or customs.

Runaway cynicism is not to blame for the resistance, nor should it be. Cynicism is not born into a society over time; it merely becomes active when it's triggered. That's nature's way of saying that something is wrong. The more indifferent people become to the warning produced by nature, the more susceptible they become. The effect this has on human nature will also affect human action. By excluding the negative effect something has and replacing it with an application of diversity and tolerance, we only lend passage to more acceptance.

Tolerance tells us to permit a nuisance or pain. It means to take in the beliefs and conduct of others without judgment or opinion of action performed. No sane or rational people would allow any such action to gain entry. When the body's immune system is no longer able to resist what's slowly killing it, it's because an outside force has entered inside the body and taken over. The same can be said about our physical environment. When we've allowed ourselves to be so overcome that we can no longer resist something that's foreign or unnatural to our environment, we simply die off by capitulating and adapting to the harmful and invasive organism. Unless a proper defense mechanism is put into place, utilized, and maintained, a passive aggressive opposition will play its hand and the inevitable will occur. The more tolerance is shouted about and insisted upon, demand will only increase with appeasement. Continuing to feed a hungry animal will only ensure its return for more.

Language is an art and can be the most destructive weapon that man can possess. It shares equal power whether it's dividing the masses or assembling its forces. Language is a centralized weapon with its own built-in database. It receives feedback when its message has gotten through to its intended destination. A response, whether positive or negative, always means that communication has been made. Never in the history of the world has a path to victory been laid without sending, receiving, or exchanging information in some way. Anytime you want to add, subtract, or alter someone's thinking, it requires transporting of information. How far a person is moved in terms of emotion solely depends on the data and its presentation.

They don't necessarily have to understand the data; it only has to be accepted into the mind. The knowledge that's obtained by people through communication can be used to influence them to be in favor of or against something. In any event, the more widely known something is, the more likely it is to spread and propagate. The important thing to point out is that people are not nearly concerned with how something happened, only that it happened because of what or who. The general population are, for the most part, simply too lazy to do any kind of research.

We also live in a blame culture, which serves as a convenient addition to the fact. Most humans need and want to have a reason for their unfortunate situation because, without it, they would bear some responsibility.

This is called a blame epidemic. This has been used as a tactic on ordinary people for thousands of years.

Throughout history, we've seen it played time and again, from Alexander the Great to Charlemagne. Mark Anthony in 45 B.C. relied on the people's sympathy in order to kill off the senate and put his triumvirate in power.

The same concept is being applied today: "Give me your tired, your poor and huddled masses yearning to breathe free." In other words, you're doing without because the undeserving have more than they should. Now, with an oath and a pledge of loyalty, I can make your life what it should be. History has proven that all people really need is a little hope and a promise; that's all they really need to follow someone into an abyss or otherwise. Ever since man was created he's struggled with the temptation to try and gain more. Whether it was with an apple or an empire, people can be led through any garden or across any continent with the right words.

# CHAPTER 35
# VERBAL EUGENICS

When their belief system collapses, people panic. Most of them don't know where to go or what to think. That is, until someone offers them something to hold on to. When people have a standard they can follow, they're no longer required to think. They can just repeat learned information that's been dispensed. Humans will do or say almost anything to improve their quality of life. With the right technique, they can be led in any direction with little effort. You only have to offer something that appeals to their senses. If it looks good, you have their eyes. If it sounds good, you have their ears, and that means that they're listening; that means something is desired, and that puts people in motion.

This can all be made possible with what I call verbal eugenics. It's a pleasant concordance of sound that appeals to its listeners, who, in time, will rally around it. It's easy to be elegant and take command of a stage if you're asking all of the questions that need to be asked. You don't even need to answer the questions that are asked. The objective should be to answer the questions that should have been asked. Everyone already knows that no one plots a good deed for anyone, so people are naturally reluctant to involve themselves. They are hesitant and that means that there is an element of fear. When people belong to something much larger than themselves, they become part of it. It is then that they're more inclined to stand for a belief.

Imitation is the most sincere form of flattery. Therefore, human nature compels a person to reflect what they take interest in and become part of.

That means that they're inspired by something. When emotion inspires someone, they also want the ability to rise as high as their passion. Instead, we have widespread disappointment and inexplicable rage. The consensus is that everyone's suffering, trying to overcome, or coping to see how much they can endure. How long should you hold out and suffer in silence?

Evolution does not change everything. Some things are going to remain the same until a structural change is made. That means that you either strike while the iron is hot or remain set in purpose. It's not an all-or-nothing proposal. It is always easier to abandon all logic and reason than to remain in the same state. That's why so many people choose to keep the same brand they have. They're simply afraid of what else the change may bring with it.

It's true that most change does not come without hardship, but in the end, you usually end up with something more. Change is good more often than not; without it where would you be? When you change something, you're really exchanging one thing for another. So why would you not swap a continuous difficulty for one that will most likely improve your current circumstances? By doing this, you apply logic and reason, then use it to your own advantage. The malcontent will try mauling you in a public venue. This will be especially true as the notoriety builds. That is why a close process of observation and thought will play such a pivotal role in the mass meeting. When you strike a chord, you want it to resonate and be well-received among the hearers. Logic and reason will strengthen the continuity of the message.

When it becomes evident that certain causes have certain results, the conclusions can then be derived from the leading principle that's being given. This is why the masses will gather under the tent where this Aristotelian logic and reason is preached—it makes sense to them. When something makes sense, people become more aware of their surroundings. There is now a conscious perception derived through the senses. You have now given them the ability to judge their external conditions with a new sense of direction.

How is all of this made possible? Through careful exhortation of the facts. Humans are really quite docile creatures, so when an earnest speech is addressed to the minds and hearts of the listeners, it can be very persuasive. After that, there only needs to be a little incentive for participation to commence. It's hard to catch anything unless you put a line in the water. When you bait your hook with your heart, the fish will bite. Then, all it takes is a little logic and Socratic dialectical reasoning to make it happen.

It's called the Art of Reasoning Process. That's where the truth and validity of a theory or opinion is examined by question and answer with rhetoric or argument. In other words, you ask the questions and give the answers to whom you're speaking. It really becomes quite systematic when you know the subject matter. You already know the problem, now you only have to spell out the solution in a way they can understand it. This is what I call tempering. You start out with small amounts, being careful not to go to the extreme. You don't want to overdose your audience, so you allow them to build up a tolerance to your dialogue. The other important point is to never reveal everything that's baked into the cake.

# CHAPTER 36
# SOCIAL WARFARE

**M**an by definition is ambivalent and circumspect by nature. It should be a source of pleasure to give society something that in return helps you dispose of something unworthy. The odds of a negative effect will always increase, not because we don't know what to do, but because we don't do what we already know. Seeing what everyone else sees and thinking what no one else has thought is a lit candle.

A candle loses nothing by lighting another candle. In the end, it doesn't really matter if we get credit for our ideas as long as they're used. Far more will be accomplished when we don't care who gets the credit or where it goes.

There is no dichotomy between right and wrong. When new facts emerge, we have to be prepared to change our thinking. We can only bury things for so long. In other words, what goes down will eventually come up. Even then, nothing just keeps geometrically going up. Every moment of our lives is travel in one direction or another.

Fulfilled potential is a rational emotion. In many cases, it helps to fuel motivation we lack. The heaviest burden we carry is usually having nothing to carry at all. No one really knows their social limitations until their imagination has been challenged. A major challenge is what ordinary people are forced by their circumstances to confront. That's when the right words to others can be highly effective and persuasive, especially to those who are in a state of agitation. When a person's theory is killed by a fact, they are devastated, largely because they were not cautiously optimistic to begin with.

They suddenly realize that they've been hammering a cold iron. When we're depending solely on ourselves and the time comes to forgo an advantage, it's then that we find where our strength lies. We then have an obligation to ourselves to explore what all possibilities are. The struggle will always end up being the prize. Holding on will be pivotal in a time of crisis.

History teaches us that the best laid plans of mice and men can easily go astray and often do. Never for a minute should we allow ourselves to think that it can't happen here. When people continue to ingest poison, it's certain to disagree with them sooner or later. The mind has the capability to absorb the poison with no immediate effect, unlike the body that quickly exhibits symptoms.

We are not a cohesive nation, and few people care about what's going on in another place at any given moment. So, when the time comes, will we all rise from the ashes like a phoenix? Or will we simply capitulate without any resistance? There are few circumstances so unfortunate that a skillful mind cannot withdraw some advantage from them. Instead of seeing the glass as half full or half empty, we should find out that it's neither. The glass is simply too large for its contents and more can be added.

Each day is a renewal, whether we choose to admit it or not. The mind has the remarkable ability to heal as well as kill, depending on what's fed into it. Even the most ardent would concur, the mind can be a powerful weapon. By nature, humans want something to be what they think. And for practical purposes, that's often what it becomes. Still, no matter how instrumental we may become in our efforts, at the end of the day, the more knowledge you end up with will reduce you in some degree to a humble human.

No matter how resistant or impervious one may become, our nature sometimes prevails over our mind. Never think that we only understand what is subjective. Without objective knowledge, you can't keep up with logic.

There has to be a certain amount of objective knowledge in the world in which you live. Otherwise there would be nowhere for anyone to begin.

Western civilization was built on objective reasoning. Without logic and reason there would be no science or civilization. Anytime we think that all knowledge is not relative, it puts reason under attack. Reason gives us the ability to think, understand, and draw conclusions. It also gives us a good sense of judgment of what is practical and possible.

Objective knowledge is the basis on which things are built. When we're not influenced by personal feelings, we can see outside our environment. We don't know who discovered water, but we're all quite sure it wasn't a fish. That means when you've always lived in the same environment, you never really know what that environment means until you've been removed. In order for something to be understood, it has to be in mind or memory as a result of experience or learning.

# CHAPTER 37
# WITHOUT LOGIC THERE CAN BE NO REASON

A Machiavellian decision has to be made. Those who love you will love you; those who hate you will hate you. That means that things are not yet done, and that's why we are obviously, quantifiably engulfed in chaos. The goal of observation is to make objective and precise observations of realistic behavior. To better understand something, you must begin with your own senses and perceptions. Instead, we now have a perceptional shift in society. Mindfulness requires situational awareness in order to make rational decisions. The benefit will always be the outcome, especially when you can understand the transient nature of things. Reason alone can provide someone with knowledge, but reason alone will not be enough. So, now I think, therefore I am something, so I have reason to exist. That is part of the reasoning process. Now that you have existence, essence will follow soon after through the manner of conduct.

People acquire knowledge through demonstration and deductive argument. It's clear how people can acquire new knowledge from a previous example. By doing this you begin the process of unraveling a mind in order to focus a mind. With the right technique, get inside the head, magnify the problem, and present the solution. Thereby you can easily and more readily turn a nonconformist into a conformist. The mind of man has been pulled into the gutter because of what he sees and hears. It is for this reason alone that society is in a downward spiral.

Brilliant minds are polluted and told how to think without a presentation of facts, thereby making effective intervention difficult. Sometimes you have to go out of your sphere of influence in order to get into someone's head. Even with this Machiavellian approach, at the end of the day, those who love you will remain and those who hate you will continue to hate you. It's the way of all things. Not only is there an answer for all things, but there is a reason for everything. Effective intervention is highly unlikely without reason. When reason occurs, the answer will always follow. Reason alone gives you nearly unlimited opportunity to demonstrate cause and effect. People do not really have to understand the cause to know the effect it's having. They only have to be able to read the data, not understand it.

# CHAPTER 38

# DUPLICITY

Sometimes the only way to convince people that we're sincere about something is by displaying self-sacrifice. Being willing to let go of something in order to make a situation better or more profitable doesn't mean that we have to let go of our moral principles. We live in a society that's seething with cultural decay. There always seems to be a complaint when someone else is doing better than another person. People have come to think that the only way to get ahead is through attrition because all other roads lead to perdition.

There's always someone creating a social disorder with an accolade, telling other people that they're out of step, when, in fact, they are the ones out of step with reality. We live in a time when, more than ever, people want to tell the system that they no longer desire to be in the shadows. When someone is a passive participant in something, they often fail to realize that they are still a participant. We have become a society where people are quick to tell someone else that they're wrong without even knowing the facts.

One of the first basic rules of science is that you never close the door to evidence that is presented to you without examining it first. There are no absolutes in science, no matter the circumstances. Figuratively speaking, when a person has contempt about something, there will always be an appearance of impropriety. History teaches us that irreverence appeals to a dominant person and admission leads to conquest. We usually see only what people want us to see when they project an image of themselves.

More often than not, it's only a feign display or a fleeting image of social evolution slipping past our eyes.

There are demographic examples in everything, especially when it comes to dealing with living entities. There is a dynamic process that enhances a state of consensus and awareness. We operate under a state of consciousness and awareness where we see ourselves as what we want to be instead of what we truly are. From the outside looking in, it's easy for people to define us not only by our actions but also by our inactions.

Fear is an obstacle that we sometimes allow to turn into an illusion. It sometimes becomes necessary in life to be aggressive in order to move forward. Everyone wants to be free from hysteria or the fear that's in their mind. No one wants the trepidation or the paranoia of walking into a jungle and thinking that every animal wants to eat them. Mankind has learned through experience that silence terrifies people more than anything.

More people don't want to take a leap into the unknown because they're afraid of change. We have evolved to the point that we are always depending on someone somewhere to persuade and invoke change. People want to put their hope and trust in someone to give them something different or better without the fear of whatever change may come about in the process. We're inherently and historically opposed to any new idea from anyone whom we may have any uncertainty about, especially if they do not immediately appeal to our interest or our intellect.

There is always something suspect about anyone who inspires and appeals to the masses with a broad message of something new, different, or better. The reason is that it's in our nature to only envelop ourselves in the things we're confident will improve our existing or current circumstances. From time to time, we have to do away with our assumptions of duplicity in things in order for new ideas to emerge and take root. In order for people to flourish, prosper, and keep up with progress, they must be willing to undergo change when the time comes.

# CHAPTER 39
# SELF-PRESERVATION 2

The first stage of subversion is demoralization. As human beings we have to realize that we did not descend from the zoological order. We're all connected to other people, even ones we hate. We're all part of the same ecosystem, and if we allow the system to be poisoned, we're all going to get sick. Some minds are already so sick and polluted that they can't be reached.

Slow extinction from apathy is indifference and lacks understanding. When we water down standards for the sake of diversity, we end up losing both. People have to be persuaded before they can be instructed on anything, including extremists. Intolerance is the worst thing about extremists. When someone is completely intolerant they become hollowed out inside and nature abhors a vacuum.

Fanatical people redouble their efforts to do something even when it's effortless to do so. There is little to no state of reasoning, only a state of mind. There's a cost-benefit ratio to everything. The greatest difficulty and risk comes when we have the freedom to do what we want. It's usually the ones who are the loudest about their rights who don't want others to have the right to say what they don't want to hear.

Life doesn't owe anything to anyone, and it's usually people who are not satisfied that are expecting too much of something anyway. People are generally more upset about someone else's wealth than their own poverty. It's like caring about the opinion of a person that you don't care for. Everyone is sure about certain people having an inferiority complex because it helps them think that they don't have one themselves.

An optimist facing a difficult opportunity will take it as an opportune difficulty. Loss is simply what we have once possessed. Nobody wins every time they roll the dice. It's a revolving door, we take risk in life and we give things up when we lose. It's the armies that stay in their own fort that have already lost. They are rearranging the deck chairs on the Titanic while the ice is scraping against the hull, popping out the rivets. The average person needs something enthusiastic to motivate them because a satisfied mind usually has low expectations and a lot of insensitivity. Since the creation of man, people have been playing the victim in order to take the focus off of themselves. More than anything else, people want other people to maintain the good opinion they have of themselves. The best way to get that is to make them think that it is to their advantage to do so. Being content is only a matter of temperament.

# CHAPTER 40
# TRUTH TO POWER

A principle is something that you have accepted or a moral guide as to how you're going to act. It's often associated with a change in direction. When you have a debt of human service, you have an obligation to a moral responsibility. Maintaining a principle requires consistency. We're all part of the human condition and most of us walk in the fabled shadow of selective morality. Through personal vexation, our standards deviate and undergo change.

As the environment around us changes, we change with it. No person is going to practice what they preach 100 percent of the time. That doesn't necessarily make you a hypocrite—it merely makes you human. Rarely ever does moral order take on loyalty to the community anywhere in the world.

Common philosophy teaches that all reality can be reduced to a single principle or substance. If we believe that, we could call it energy. Having control over your own energy is an art unto itself. It helps to define who you are. You have the capacity to overcome whatever the opposition may be. It's a matter of influencing and convincing your own character. That will require truth to power, which needs energy to fuel moral strength. Good intentions rarely amount to anything useful when they're not for your personal agenda.

When your primary focus is on what you can control, far more will be accomplished. That means you should regulate your intentions to better suit reality, instead of trying to regulate reality to fit the concept. Any attribute to an immoral act will result in a decrease of its intensity. For that matter, any act, whether it be morally justified or not, must be ascribed to a cause. This is especially true if it's symbolic in nature to what may already be appealing to passive spectators. To have the ability to bring objectives into focus and attack other people, there has to be a necessary incentive involved. When people are in a state of need or if they think they are in a state of need, they are usually dependent on someone or something that's provided by someone somewhere.

The provider can easily stipulate terms and conditions. Simple minds are easily entertained. The greater the spectacle, the more docile the masses become. By and large, people want to be insulated from the reality of life and to think the world as they know it, and all its shortcomings, could be recreated. That would bring nearly any amount of sacrifice or loyalty to the table. The self-appointed, downtrodden, well-wishing deniers of reality are easily taken in. Their already hypothetical attitudes make communication less demanding on the recipient and on the one who is imparting instruction.

Language is a powerful instrument used for communication. When ideas go from words to deeds, it quickly and easily entails a right or an obligation from its source. For example, a person who makes use of others for a moral purpose is simply devising a method that's producing a desired effect for the good. You're only an object that's used in serving a purpose. Therefore, you're pragmatic and there's a means to your action that, in turn, brings moral justification. When you commit to something, you bind or pledge allegiance with emotional adherence in some way.

Whether it's social in theory or in action, it must carry with it a driving force. You not only have to be the power behind it, but you have to be part of it as well. Pragmatism will test the truth and examine its consequences. It relates to the state of affairs, therefore it is relative and not speculative. A fundamental assumption cannot be depended upon when making an observation, in order to give an accurate description of reason. When the attention of the listeners is diverted from a material to a moral prospective, there will be the accompanying roar because reason has been brought into play.

Far less incentive is required when people have reason to commit to something. It's an age-old method that's withstood the test of time for centuries. When people are made aware of why their current state of affairs are so unfortunate, miserable, and unacceptable, they have listened to the voice of reason, which now has the ability to persuade the multitude of hearers. When there has been a recognition of reality, people are largely inclined to follow a plan of recourse. That in itself will include taking possession of a normal condition of prosperity as opposed to the alternative. They've plugged into a matrix that's now a public alliance.

# CHAPTER 41
# DECEPTION

It's quite common for people without any sign of intelligence to say things in a skillful language. They use a silk tongue to con the world into thinking they are something they're not. This is more commonly done through word manipulation. Its main purpose is to distort reality and cause confusion, therefore making people more susceptible to what's being said.

When a person controls the meaning of the words, they can cleverly control the people who use the words. It's called the art of sedition, and it's a technique that's been practiced for centuries. Create the problem and the solution in order to manipulate and control the masses.

A society can always be trained to do the bidding of its leaders. The principle seems obvious that people have become dimly aware of their surroundings. When people are told that they are being treated unfairly and under attack, it becomes easy to undermine them because they already have a distorted outlook on something. This is especially true when someone else is pushing the mantra to weaken and lead them down a false road. When someone has been gorging on something for a long time, they're going to have a hard time giving it up. Once someone reaches their own epiphany of a must-have mentality, it becomes much harder to let something go.

It turns into a mental and physical game because they are battling their own prerequisite. At some point it becomes necessary for a person to ask why they have so much enmity. In terms of social insanity, they have been falsely using the struggle of material deprivation to advance their narrative.

A logical conclusion would be they have a wherewithal outlook and a false provocation.

In order to become stronger, a person has to learn to let something go. If we want better things in life, we sometimes have to give something up. People have allowed themselves to become completely vociferous in what they are inferring, mainly because they've become immune to reality. To cut someone out or cut them off and beat them should not be the object of conversation.

The object of conversation should be to converse about what we're inferring. That's what an advanced civilized society does. When we speak or act too quickly, we're most likely to make a mistake. There is always going to be diversity, no matter where we go. We're always going to encounter pain and defeat every so often, because no one is exempt from reality. Therefore it can't be avoided. Just because someone is sure they are doing the right thing, that doesn't give them an insurance policy against misfortune. Good intentions can only give someone merit and peace of mind by way of self-worth and dignity.

At some point, we have to all decide to look through the clear lenses of reality and accept what we see. Even when we think it's meaningless and insignificant to do so.

# CHAPTER 42
# DECEPTION 2

We have to be willing to admit facts even when they hurt. Life is not going to give anyone what they want every second of the day. Truth is not always relative. We're all guilty of yielding to thoughtless impulse, and many times the answer is in the outcome. Sometimes we don't know the answer to something until we're tested. People have confused what's futile with what's popular. Usually when a person keeps telling themselves the same things over and over, they eventually sell themselves a bill of goods. As a matter of recourse, they parse their answers, despite their deficiencies, and instead of overcoming, they create more issues.

There's an art to cultivating what's inside a person. It's okay to use freedom of expression to some extent, even to the people we despise. However, when we rush to judgment, we usually walk away from any collective understanding. We can't express everything in words and often we betray ourselves for vanity's sake. It's in a preserved state of perpetual puerility we inadvertently leave things behind, especially our allegiance to something. Ignorance in action is restricting our social conscience and believing in something we're not. Even in the most sophisticated society, people are willing to settle for complete ignorance in order to get what they want.

Nearly everyone can be led to believe the lie they want to be true. It's hard for a person to take pleasure believing in something when they're bewildered. When we deny allegations, it's also necessary to defy the accuser. Anyone who acts so clean, innocent, and neutral usually ends up being just the opposite. It's these very people who are so high on visceral hatred who usually end up being a smear artist themselves. If someone hates something, it demonstrates that they take it seriously.

Being tolerant will, in nearly all cases, end up being used against a person. One should not be tolerant to someone who has no self-respect or self-esteem, nor should they. They've lived their whole life tearing away at the rest of society, yet they want everyone else to tolerate them. They're some of the worst people on the planet, yet they were not born that way. Miserable ideas have to be taught. There's an art to assaulting someone's mind space, especially when posing as a benign participant. That is why it can be easy to survive an external enemy, but an enemy within silently preys on the fearful. The ones who volunteer to carry the burden of others are the very ones they want to deceive.

It's impossible to successfully advance a narrative that no one supports. That's why deception is the cornerstone of the entire building process. When people are handed knowledge about something, it makes them feel smart. When someone thinks they're smart, they feel better about themselves; they no longer feel completely inferior. A new sense of pride has emerged from what they've been hearing. All the while they've been a soundboard and have no idea how to use the knowledge that's been fed to them from a congenital liar. Anyone who asserts that the truth will always triumph in the end is lying to themselves.

There is no one who will just come to us with all of the ameliorations we're looking for. More often than not, when we're looking for an answer, we have to knock hard because life can be deaf. A syllogism can be found in the most unlikely places. A moral uplift, whether sought or unsought, is only as good as the foundation upon which it's built. Being overly rigid can be counterproductive, so listening can be beneficial to the mind of the intuitive. No matter how advanced a society becomes, there is always a divide between reality and unreality because some people base their beliefs on things as they know them, but not as they want them.

By and large, people have been compromised and conquered because they simply have submitted to a false pretense. No matter what occurs, it is the same people who will continue to believe that it occurred according to a theory they've been given. Language is a pedigree of nations in the pomposity of superiority, and it's essential for people to depend on a belief that's being constantly driven.

A contortionist will always twist the facts in order to advance their narrative. They have no logic, only stating their worldly views is correct. For someone else to successfully dictate the terms, everyone has to think alike, with no small pockets of internal resistance. Any tragedy that occurs must bear no relation to their preconceived ideas or their origin. In the final analysis, it will always be the mess the tragedy makes that destroys us, not the tragedy itself.

# CHAPTER 43
# POWER TO THE PEOPLE

The people should be the ultimate power of any society when there's a modern-day battleground with a vital struggle to being intellectually enlightened and culturally enriched. It's the greatest gift that can be offered to the republic. There has to be general knowledge among the people, otherwise they will just settle for the familiar and ignore the substance. We are in danger of becoming a national institution where everyone is hysterical about the aggregate.

The pace we take and our emphasis on efficiency discourages grappling with real issues. When people are enlightened, the tyranny and oppressions of the mind start to disappear. Instead of cursing the darkness, one has to light a candle.

No one is just going to ride in and save someone for no apparent reason. A person can do something more often because they think they can. The emotional construct becomes 'I think, therefore I am.' How far someone is willing to go usually depends upon what they expect to get from the efforts.

With this sense of gain comes understanding. Whether it's internal or external, strength comes from an indomitable will.

Throwing light over the mind of the people will only move civilization from ignorance to enlightenment; then from apathy to responsibility. We have to know where the red, yellow, and green lights are. When the mind functions with Aristotelian logic, it can decipher what's real and what's not. We don't always have to put our face in the food in order to know where it came from. There has to be some analysis, because without it an imposition is created. No one has to be an expert in any field to know the data. They only need to know how to read the data. So when an entire citadel of reason has been torn apart and the data is all that's left, it then becomes necessary to prepare and want what we're preparing for.

There's always a wave of information and technological change coming. That makes for a constant race between information and catastrophe. People like to think that they generate their own life, and in many ways they do, however no one ever really has full control of their own ship. We can set our own heading, but more often than not, good ideas are destroyed. Every action we take is a compromise at some point. Everything we accept has something we give up eventually as part of a settlement. There's always something halfway between opposite opinions or course of action. By chasing two rabbits we allow them both to escape, thereby ending up with nothing.

The way we think things ought to be is highly improbable. Rather, a more influential person belonging to a place and forming a group, has greater ability to be effective. Crisis always brings out a version of someone. Either we help make something happen or we watch and do nothing.

We give up power by thinking that we don't have any. All people really need is the incentive and motivation to be lead in any direction. Suggestions that we give to someone should be for our own benefit as well. Acting indifferent is an art, making the recipient think it's their own advice that's being carried out. When we allow fear to be an imposition, we're surrendering our will power to enslavement. When a dog is running toward someone, the first thing they should do is whistle at it. There's a difference in having power and control over something. In order to know the difference, we have to delegate and be decisive. It's important to separate the two in order to know the difference.

What some see as virtue is tearing down what others believe in. It's always the individuals with a very poor neurological matrix who weaponize this action to garner power. This works only when people bury the impulse that scares them. Then, eventually the people will have no control over what's going on around them, and it will become survival of the fittest. What many fail to realize is that the underlying idea on which something is based is its foundation. And when the foundation of any structure is made weak and unstable, the supporting framework and essential parts will fall once kicked in. There can be no dichotomy in a rational opposition.

In order to look at the focal point and the vexation leading up to something, we can't skip the very beginning. Look at what has sustained mankind for the ages: taking what's forbidden, acting on what we're compelled to believe and passing the blame. Then it begs the question: whose fault is it that we live in a blame culture? Out of all living things on Earth, only humans have the instinct to lay blame on another. It comes at a greater threat to the social order today, when we allow others to invent a concept and promote it as fact with little or no opposition.

It's mostly because people no longer recognize what's a threat to social stability. We all have instincts and can hear the rumbling coming. We have DNA passed down through countless years of evolution. Even the birds know to fly away before the hurricane comes. The rest of the animals know to get out of the forest when the rumbling starts. Hosea 8:7 tells us, "For they have sown the wind and they shall reap the whirlwind." If we believe that, and we know the seeds of destruction have already been sown, then we must know that there's a whirlwind coming.

Most of us don't need a Bible to tell us what not to do unless we've already been deceived. People are generally deceived in masses. It's then that the mind becomes enslaved and the body follows. It's the defining characteristics of a seemingly benign republic. Anytime someone moves in any particular direction, it's an indicator that a decision has been made. Regardless of the direction, we're constantly stepping on a plane either going up or down.

With the continuing cry of equality, society will continue to descend into civil unrest. When the civil unrest shows its inefficacy and the people remain oblivious to what's happening and impervious to the facts, there's little chance then to disarm hostility and civil unrest will descend into civil war.

# CHAPTER 44
# PEOPLE ARE OFTEN DECEIVED IN MASSES

It's easy to confuse what we see when we're looking through a microscope. Either our lens has become cloudy or we're looking at the wrong slide, and it can be a state of dizziness for some of us. Some people have been a shill for unreality for so long that their brain is bent around how self-satisfaction feels when they think they're right. A person can easily speak the vernacular and still have a blind eye to the differential of the world.

It begs the question, why have people become so vicarious that they can't see what they've become or who they are? They have resistance fatigue to the point that they've become triangulated and refuse to accept reality. People have gotten so used to being negative for the sake of negativity that they don't know how to act when they're handed something good.

This is why we should have a robust agenda in order to stay on track. To raise the morale of people, it is essential for someone to raise the citizenry. It takes only one degree of separation to move a wide chasm. When navigating a ship, any sudden or abrupt movement can change the whole course of a heading. Whether our course is a positive or a negative one, someone somewhere will always tell us that we're wrong.

We're either doing something because it sounds good or we're doing it for a good reason. Either way, we are always at greater risk through weakness than through calculation. Discovery usually starts with thinking of what no one has thought of yet. We can't wait to learn about geology when the earthquake is over.

# CHAPTER 45
# ASSESSMENT

**W**e live in a headline world, and headline people are the easiest to manipulate. We've all become guilty of our priorities because we are most concerned with whatever the social issue of the day is. People no longer live with moral judgment and no longer recognize a trend of consequences with a clear and present danger to humanity. The only thing really shocking to anyone anymore is the truth. Nearly everyone wants to buy in and take part in the narrative without ever pursuing the facts. Actions then have consequences, because truth takes action and the consequences follow.

People primarily concern themselves in believing things that no other society in the history of mankind has ever believed. History teaches us that there's a time to let things happen and a time to make things happen. A person has to have a big enough mental stomach to eat more than a bite of reality at a time. More than anything else, people are held back by their own trepidation. Constant fear and worry is like paying interest in advance on something that we're never going to own. We become counterproductive without even realizing it.

Civilization is a continuum, so anything that extends continuously has someone on the other end doing the pushing, whether it's right or wrong. If someone cares enough about something to keep it going, they're going to want to preserve it. That means that interpretation can mean everything. No matter what the outcome is, there will always be someone who thinks that it happened according to theory. Yet somehow, people always seem to be surprised by the things they expected to happen. It's always the theory that decides what is observed rather than the facts. Anytime we believe ourselves to be possessors of the absolute, we only degrade ourselves to some degree.

When we're totally in lockstep with a theory that we've imprisoned ourselves inside it, we're like dead tissue that refuses to decompose. Our thought process is based on rearranging the things that we don't like instead of getting rid of them and putting in something different. When we suddenly understand something that we've known our whole life, we realize that we've learned something. Yet by nature people want to condemn what they cannot understand. Then by doing so, we evolve into a society that welcomes the disruptive force of candor with no vested interest in the outcome. Few people clearly know what they want. Most can't even think rationally on what they hope for. And yet, for some reason, the same people find it consoling to find that someone else's problems are greater than our own.

# CHAPTER 46
# EMPATHY

Art has been used to corrupt mankind for centuries. Music and art control and influence the mind. If we don't understand what art is in the course of events, we don't understand art. The advantage of the unjust is more apparent, and the individuals that refuse to participate in the unjust are the most miserable. One has to ask, 'what is the ideal society we are trying to achieve, and what is the master plan?' How have we as a nation gotten so off base that we need objective reality to rediscover our own values?

You can rally people who are blind to your own will in order to advance your cause, but in the final analysis, you can't have a reasonable discussion with people who object to objective facts. You can't inject character just by being around someone or some people. Initially, you have to instill peace between individual groups and society. The city and the nation are the soul of society.

Whether we choose to agree with it or not, Plato had a plan. First, we have to realize when modes of music and art change, the fundamental laws of man change with it, so it becomes necessary to bring people down to reality. In the end, we realize that we're not all the same. When a person uses a single emotion to reach people, they will lose the people's attention. When someone is in their own sandbox playing by their own rules, it becomes easier to embolden other people and enable them to do what they want to do.

Sometimes it becomes necessary to undertake our own analysis of the obvious even when it seems insignificant to do so. If we like someone, we usually listen to them to see if what they say makes sense. If we don't like someone and we're listening to them, it's only because we're waiting for them to slip and fall off of their high wire.

It takes a really active participant to engage and manipulate the mind of other people to make them think certain things are okay. Sometimes the talker is addicted to talking, while the listener becomes addicted to listening. We formulate our thoughts and express our thoughts, and we seek answers in our own way trying to avoid the questions. There are not a lot of people who see reality for what it is, and those who do are usually not willing to express the reality when they do see it.

There is a positive criticism and there is a negative criticism. We have to learn to separate the two and internalize our rage instead of taking it out on other people. Everything in life is a strategy, no matter which direction we choose to go. People like hearing distasteful things about other people because it makes them aware of themselves. All people are flawed in one way or another. All our interior world has evolved in such a way that if a person decides to criticize someone else for doing something wrong, people will automatically accuse that person of being judgmental and being prejudiced. It's a strange dichotomy, and more so now it has become the way the average person thinks and sees things.

# CHAPTER 47
# ENEMIES WITHOUT ENMITY

People are enslaved in lives they loathe. More than anything else, they want a measure of stability, yet we inherently sow the seeds of our own demise. There is always a consequence to any behavior, no matter the motive. It's part of the human condition. It may become necessary to learn, unlearn, and relearn what we think. Humans typically have a stronger impulse for negative than positive. Life is a mardi gras devised by the devil, and it can't be reasoned with or tricked. Anytime we try to reason with nature, we always end up losing, and it always has a way of getting even. We always learn best when we are able to hear, see, feel, and taste a concept. There's always a big audience for reality. People can taste it when it's their own food, their own wine, beer, tea, etc.

Most people have safely resigned themselves to accepting reality. No fundamental part of society relies on a nostrum for their stability. By nature, we want to know more and say more, but without a voice, all we have left is physicality. A person can always judge their performance based on how they feel after the fact. Negative emotions are usually more powerful than positive emotions. There's no such thing as a poor emotion. The more we subdue our emotions, the more negative they become. Then we become our own enemy without enmity. Even when someone is unwilling to learn, they can still be made to think and come to a better knowledge of their own potential.

People are searching for a catalyst. They often have to be brought to life and given an identity in order to move forward. They are more easily directed by only what amuses their minds. They have to be pursued with ardor and attended to with diligence. When calling upon other people, it's necessary to let them know that they are needed and not just wanted, and without them, you have unattainable goals with inadequate tools.

Fatigue will always be a price of leadership, and the irony of punishment comes with it. The more it's used to gain control, the less influence it will bring. Goals, needs, and motives must be first taken into account within any endeavor. Napoleon bankrupted France fighting constant wars. We do the same by not channeling our negative impulse, thereby not acquiring a greater opportunity.

# CHAPTER 48
# ANALYTICAL

Few of us have truly outstanding gifts. We have to accept the fact that someone else may be better at something than we are. We should never cut ourself off from constructive advice just because we don't like who the advice is coming from. If we become like the opposition, we put ourselves at a disadvantage. So what have we gained? A person has to allow themselves the ability to think clearly and be reasonable. We have to feel what's going on in the world in order to make changes in our own life.

Instead, we dilute ourselves by saying it can't happen here or it can't happen to me. At some point, a person has to stop and take an analytical view of life and look at what's happening and see the magnitude of the potential ramifications. There is no absolutely perfect system, just as there are no absolutes in science. When we appeal and adhere only to the same group of people who support the same thing over and over without change, we start to glorify the past and devalue the present. When we find new opportunities, we often find new dangers, so we don't necessarily get rid of our problems, we just trade them in for new ones.